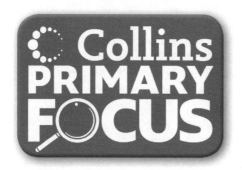

Spelling

Introductory Teacher's Guide

Joyce Vallar and Carol Doncaster

William Collins' dream of knowledge for all began with the publication of his first book in 1819. A self-educated mill worker, he not only enriched millions of lives, but also founded a flourishing publishing house. Today, staying true to this spirit, Collins books are packed with inspiration, innovation and practical expertise. They place you at the centre of a world of possibility and give you exactly what you need to explore it.

Collins. Freedom to teach.

Published by Collins
An imprint of HarperCollins*Publishers* Ltd.
77–85 Fulham Palace Road
Hammersmith
London
W6 8JB

Browse the complete Collins catalogue at
www.collinseducation.com

10 9 8 7 6 5 4 3 2

ISBN: 978-0-00-742660-7

British Library Cataloguing in Publication Data
A Catalogue record for this publication is available from the British Library.

Cover template: LCD
Cover illustration: Q2A Media
Series design: Neil Adams and Garry Lambert
Illustrations: Lynda Murray, Sascha Lipscomb, James Walmesley, Gwyneth Williamson

Printed and bound by Hobbs the Printers, UK.

MIX
Paper from
responsible sources
FSC™ C007454
www.fsc.org

Contents

Welcome to *Collins Primary Focus: Spelling*

Accurate spelling is one of the keys to children becoming fluent and effective writers. Competent spellers need to spend less time thinking about spelling, enabling them to channel their thoughts and energy into composing the text, varying the sentence structure and choosing words effectively.

This new edition of *Collins Primary Focus: Spelling* has been written to support teachers in implementing a whole-school spelling programme, drawing on the methodology and objectives from the Primary National Strategy and *Support for Spelling* (second edition). Clear guidance is given for investigating each spelling rule with the whole class and through group and independent work. The emphasis is on systematic and explicit teaching of spelling strategies, conventions and rules, building upon children's established phonic knowledge.

Components of the programme

Age 4+
 Introductory Practice Book A
978-0-00-752517-1
 Introductory Practice Book B
978-0-00- 752565-2
 My First Word Book
978-0-00-742708-6

Age 5+
 Introductory Practice Book 1A
978-0-00-752566-9
 Introductory Practice Book 1B
978-0-00-752567-6
 My Second Word Book
978-0-00-742709-3

Age 6+
 Introductory Pupil Book
978-0-00-742655-1
 Introductory Teacher's Guide
978-0-00-742660-7
 Introductory Practice Book
978-0-00-743094-9
 My Third Word Book
978-0-00-742710-9

Age 7+
 Pupil Book 1
978-0-00-742656-0
 Teacher's Guide 1
978-0-00-742661-4
 Practice Book 1
978-0-00-743095-6
 My Fourth Word Book
978-0-00-743153-3

Age 8+
 Pupil Book 2
978-0-00-742657-7
 Teacher's Guide 2
978-0-00-742662-1
 Practice Book 2
978-0-00-743096-3

Age 9+
 Pupil Book 3
978-0-00-742658-4
 Teacher's Guide 3
978-0-00-742663-8
 Practice Book 3
978-0-00-743097-0
My Fifth Word Book
978-0-00-743154-2

Age 10+
 Pupil Book 4
978-0-00-742659-1
 Teacher's Guide 4
978-0-00-742664-5
 Practice Book 4
978-0-00-743098-7

Teaching spelling: the theory

Learning to spell

Learning to spell is a developmental process and most children pass through five very distinct stages of spelling as they develop their own skills and strategies.

1. **Random letters**: children write down random letters to express meaning, for example, H, c, s, G.

2. **Estimated spelling**: children attempt to represent letter sounds. Attempts are semi-phonetic; there is some correspondence but vowel sounds are often omitted, for example, bs (bus), cbj (cabbage).

3. **Phonetic spelling**: children represent all the sounds in words, for example, cat, rain, sez (says). Spelling of unfamiliar known words is memorised visually.

4. **Transitional stage**: children start to rely more heavily on visual cues, recognising that some irregular words don't follow regular phonetic spelling patterns, for example, the, says, said. They make analogies with word patterns they already know, such as, time, clime (climb); shed, shef (chef).

5. **Mature stage**: correct spellings are used. Children can visualise words and have a good knowledge of conventions, word structures and rules.

The approach

The following pattern underpins the teaching and learning in *Collins Primary Focus: Spelling*.

1. **Revisit-Explain-Use**: children learn best when their next steps build on what they already know. The first part of the teaching sequence revises and consolidates prior learning and introduces new learning. Whole-class work is suggested in this section.

2. **Teach-Model-Define**: this section provides a range of direct teaching and learning activities for the whole class, including teacher modelling and involving the children in new learning. The children are invited to:

   a) identify patterns in words

   b) hypothesise and test their ideas

   c) explain the principle behind the pattern, if appropriate.

3. **Practice-Explore-Investigate**: this section gives the children the opportunity to work independently, in pairs or in small groups, using a range of activities, including the *Pupil Books*, Resource sheets and *Practice Books*, to practise and consolidate new learning. Opportunities are provided in the Enrichment section to explore and extend the rule, investigating exceptions, variations and applications.

4. **Apply-Assess-Reflect**: the final section gives the children the opportunity to reflect on what they have learned and how they feel about what they have learned.

   • Ask the children to use 'thumbs up' or 'traffic lights' to indicate how well they have understood the new learning. Their responses will determine the next steps in your teaching.

- Opportunities are given for the children to identify the key points of their learning and to apply what they have learned orally and in writing by composing their own sentences and through dictated sentences. Each unit has five **dictation** sentences. Read the sentences aloud, or ask the children to read them aloud to each other. The children should write down the words they hear, remembering the spelling rules.

- At the end of this section, it is suggested that the children add the words they have learned to their personal **Word Book**. The children can use their *Word Book* as a dictionary and a reference tool when writing.

Spelling strategies

- Good spellers search for ways in which language works and move from approximations to conventional spelling.

- Good spellers have many strategies they use to help them learn to spell.

- Memorising lists of words and learning to spell are two different processes.

Learning to spell is a complex process and children should be taught to use a variety of strategies. As children's spelling expertise increases it becomes less obvious that strategies are being applied. The spelling of a word appears automatic and only when a difficult word is encountered is the process slowed down and appropriate strategies can be observed in action.

Collins Primary Focus: Spelling encourages children to investigate spelling patterns and form successful spelling strategies.

Common strategies

- Use knowledge of phonemes – knowing the sound/symbol relationship helps children to segment words into phonemes for spelling, for example, *r – ai – n*.

- Use knowledge of onset and rime – knowing the spelling of one word can help with another, for example, came, name, same.

- Letter patterns and strings – practising common letter patterns and strings (such as *-ing*, *-tion*, *-ight*, *-ious*) helps to establish the spelling and the serial probability of letters.

- Break words into syllables – lem/on/ade.

- Use mnemonics, for example, aerial: Angry elephants ride in amber lorries.

- Find words within words – believe has a lie in it.

- Use the 'Look, Say, Cover, Write and Check' method. Children need to get into the habit of looking at words with intent: observing details, highlighting difficult parts, visualising and committing the word to memory. Children with poor visual memories may need extra support and practice in order to commit words to memory successfully.

- Proofreading for errors.

- Apply general spelling rules – see p7.

- Apply knowledge of root words, prefixes and suffixes – see the general rules on p7.

General spelling rules

- *q* is always followed by *u* in the English language.
- No English word in the English language ends in *j* or *v* (except colloquialisms, such as guv).
- In most words *i* comes before *e* (chief) except after *c* (ceiling). Use *ei* when it sounds like *ai* (neighbour).
- If nouns and verbs are formed from the same root word, the noun usually ends in *ce* and the verb in *se* (practice/practise, advice/advise).
- The sounds *ee* or *i* at the end of a word are usually represented by *y* (teddy, cry). Words don't usually end in *i* (exceptions: taxi, kiwi).

Making plurals

- To make the plural form of most nouns, just add -*s* (boat, boats).
- To make the plural of a noun that ends with -*s*, -*x*, -*sh* or -*ch* add -*es* (dish, dishes).
- To make the plural of a noun that ends in a consonant +*y*, change *y* to *i* and add *es* (library, libraries).
- To make the plural of a noun that ends in -*f*, change the *f* to *v* and add -*es* (elf, elves). If the word ends in -*fe*, drop the *fe* and add -*ves* (wife, wives).
- To make the plural of most nouns ending in vowels, just add -*s* (sofa, sofas). For some nouns ending in -*o*, add -*es* (potato, potatoes).
- Some words have irregular plurals, for example, mouse, mice.

Adding suffixes

- To add a suffix to a word with a short vowel and one consonant, double the last consonant before adding the suffix or *y* (chop, chopping, choppy).
- To add a suffix to a word with a long vowel, do not double the last consonant (rain, raining, rainy).
- To add a suffix when a word ends with -*e*, drop the *e* if the suffix begins with a vowel or is *y* (smoke, smoking, smoky). Keep the *e* if the suffix begins with a consonant (care, careful).
- To add the suffixes -*able* or -*ous* to a word that ends in -*ce* or -*ge*, keep the *e* (notice, noticeable; courage, courageous).
- To add a suffix when a word ends with -*y* (that sounds *ee*), change the *y* to an *i* before adding the suffix (happy, happiness).
- The suffixes -*ful* and -*til* have only one *l*.

Adding prefixes

- Just add the prefix to the root word.
- *Al* at the beginning of a word only has one *l*.

Glossary of terms

Auditory discrimination

The ability to hear small differences between sounds and words when listening to words or sounds presented orally. It allows us to hear the difference between similar sounds such as *d/t*, *p/b* and between similar words such as mad/mat, pan/plan.

Digraph

A digraph is the combination of two letters used to make a single speech sound such as *ch* and *ai*.

Homophone

A word that sounds the same as another but is spelled differently and has a different meaning, for example:

flour/flower   bear/bare

Homonyms

Words that share the same spelling and pronunciation but have different meanings, for example:

bank 1) noun: a business that looks after people's money
      2) noun: the raised ground along the edge of a river or lake

ring 1) verb: if you ring someone, you phone them
      2) verb: when a telephone or bell rings, it makes a clear, loud sound
      3) noun: a small circle of metal that you wear on your finger.

Letter strings

A letter string is a sequence of letters that occurs frequently, for example, *-ing*, *-igh*.

Onset and rime

Onset and rime introduces the children to the idea of word families and lays down foundations for good spelling strategies.

Onset is the initial consonant or consonant cluster of letters in words which precede the vowel, for example, *b* in bag, *cl* in clock.

Rime refers to the vowel and final consonant(s), for example, *-at* in cat, *-ing* in string; or the final digraph, for example, *-ow* in cow, how or now.

When using onset and rime, words are grouped by final sounds, for example:

man	best	new
can	vest	few
ran	nest	grew
van	test	flew
fan	pest	chew

Oral discrimination

The ability to articulate small differences in sounds and words when speaking.

Phoneme

A phoneme is the smallest unit of sound in a word. There are 44 phonemes in the English language.

A phoneme can be formed by one, two, or three letters, for example:

c as in cat	one letter
ch as in chat	two letters
igh as in high	three letters

Cat has three phonemes, <u>c</u>-<u>a</u>-<u>t</u>.

Chat also has three phonemes, <u>ch</u>-<u>a</u>-<u>t</u>.

Rhyme/rime

Rhymes and rimes are not identical. Rhymes have word endings which sound the same but are not necessarily spelled in the same way, for example, socks/fox. Rimes are word endings which always retain the same spelling pattern, for example, box/fox.

Short vowels

The five single letter vowels *a*, *e*, *i*, *o* and *u*, for example in words like cat, pet and dog.

Long vowels

Vowels that sound the same as the letter names, for example in words like cake, me and coat.

Using *Collins Primary Focus: Spelling*

The integrated resources of *Collins Primary Focus: Spelling* provide a practical, step-by-step approach to teaching spelling. A synthetic phonics approach is used at the beginning of the course and high-frequency words are used throughout. Learning is supported by examples, visual cues and differentiated practice activities.

Each of the five levels consists of a *Teacher's Guide*, a *Pupil Book*, a *Practice Book* and a *Word Book*. The *Pupil Book* and *Teacher's Guide* are divided into units. Each unit focuses on a particular spelling rule or pattern. **Progress Units** appear frequently throughout the course to facilitate assessment and consolidate learning. A **Spellchecker** challenge is presented at the end of each *Pupil Book*, encouraging children to read with care, and to check and edit the work of others as well as their own.

Collins Primary Focus: Spelling and text work

Collins Primary Focus: Spelling encourages an integrated approach to teaching spelling. Children should not think of learning to spell only during 'spelling lessons'. They must be encouraged to look for and highlight examples of spelling rules encountered when reading, and to apply their knowledge and skills when writing. To assist with this integration, the units are linked to texts in the appropriate level of *Collins Primary Literacy* (CPL).

Collins Primary Focus: Spelling and grammar work

To demonstrate the link between grammatical rules and spelling rules, units are linked to relevant grammar points in the appropriate level of *Collins Primary Focus: Grammar and Punctuation*.

Collins Primary Focus: Spelling and dictionary work

Dictionary definitions have been sourced from the *Collins Junior Illustrated Dictionary* (978-0-00-735390-3) and the *Collins Primary Illustrated Dictionary* (978-0-00-735393-4). In *Pupil Books 1–4* it is suggested that children regularly use dictionaries to check their spellings while working through the activities. Children working from the *Introductory Pupil Book* may be too young to work with dictionaries, so dictionary work is only suggested for extension activities.

A *Pupil Book* unit

The **Unit number** provides clear navigation through the book and through related components.

A **question** is posed to encourage children to think about the spelling rule they will be investigating.

The **spelling rule** is clearly explained and examples are given.

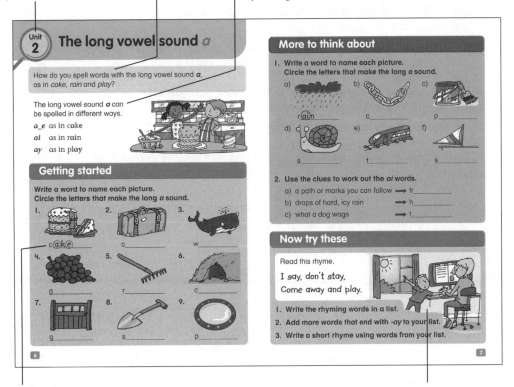

Model answers support children working without guidance.

Engaging illustrations provide visual cues to support learning.

It is important to ensure that the children can correctly identify the illustrations before starting each exercise so that there are no barriers to the learning objectives. Remind the children to read each section completely and check their understanding before they start.

Getting started

This section provides:

- activities to practise understanding of the rule
- visual cues to prompt answers.

More to think about

This section provides:

- activities to further develop understanding of the rule
- extension of the basic rule to broaden understanding.

Now try these

This section provides:

- activities to stretch and extend understanding of the rule
- opportunities to use the rule in independent writing.

A *Teacher's Guide* unit

The **Unit number** provides clear navigation through the book and through related components.

The **Unit focus** and the **Learning objectives** give the key learning outcomes for the unit.

Support for Spelling objectives are taken from the second edition of *Support for Spelling*.

Links to the **Grammar, Punctuation and Spelling Test** help you to prepare children for the end of Key Stage 2 assessment.

Collins Primary Literacy (CPL) links provide ideas for integrating spelling with text work.

Collins Primary Focus (CPF): *Grammar and Punctuation* links provide opportunities to link grammatical and spelling rules.

Dictation sentences are designed to assess the children's ability to spell words in context.

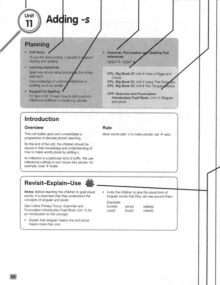

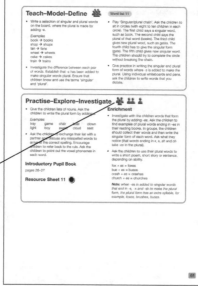

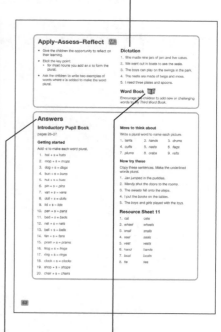

 Whole-class, group, pair and **individual** icons indicate work suitable for different classroom settings.

Answers are provided for all the activities.

The *Word Book* icon is a reminder to encourage the children to add words to their personal *Word Books*.

Clear **teacher's notes** provide step-by-step guidance for teaching the spelling rules, conventions and strategies:

- **Revisit–Explain–Use**: whole-class work to revise and consolidate prior learning

- **Teach–Model–Define**: whole-class work to introduce new learning

- **Practise–Explore–Investigate**: individual, group and pair work to practise, support, extend and investigate the learning

- **Apply–Assess–Reflect**: opportunities for children to reflect on their learning and for you to assess progress.

Resource sheets

Photocopiable resource sheets provide further opportunities for differentiated practice following on from work in the *Pupil Book*. These are ideal for group and independent work.

The following symbols have been used as a guide for differentiation:

■ activities for the less able

● activities for those of average ability

▲ activities for the more able or to provide extension

Word lists

The word lists can be used throughout each unit as a source of examples and to create spelling lists for homework.

High-frequency words

High-frequency word lists are included at the back of each *Teacher's Guide* for reference.

Practice Books

Spelling rules are reinforced in each *Practice Book* with a 'Look, Say, Cover, Write, Check' exercise and related activity on every page. 'Helper' tips are provided on every page for parents or classroom assistants. These are ideal for practice at home.

Word Books

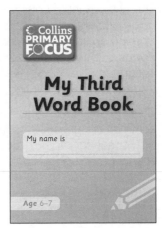

Write-in *Word Books* allow children to practise writing and spelling high-frequency words. Organised alphabetically, *My First Word Book* contains words from the first 100 high-frequency words list; *My Second Word Book* contains words from the first 100 and the next 200 high-frequency words lists; *My Third*, *Fourth* and *Fifth Word Books* contain words from the next 200 high-frequency words list. There is also plenty of space for children to add their own words for each letter of the alphabet.

Creating their own dictionary will provide experience of using reference books and give the children ownership of words they are able to recognise and use. The children should be encouraged to refer to their *Word Books* whenever they are writing, to check spellings and find interesting words. The *Word Books* could be used to create lists of words for topic work.

Assessment

There are different ways of assessing progress in children's learning.

Formative assessment

Each unit in *Collins Primary Focus: Spelling* provides opportunities for assessing reading, writing, speaking and listening skills, embedded in the everyday teaching and learning process.

Formative assessment or Assessment for Learning (AfL) is most effective when you:
• involve children in their own learning and share learning goals
• provide effective feedback to children
• adjust teaching as a result of assessment
• share with children how they can assess their own progress
• help children understand how to improve.

Summative assessment

Summative assessment is carried out periodically, for example at the end of a term, a year or a key stage. It is a judgement about children's performance at a certain point in time in relation to national standards.

Progress Units are provided within each *Pupil Book*. These units can be used for periodic assessment in a more formal setting, though it is expected that spelling would form only part of an overall assessment for levelling purposes.

A **diagnostic test** is provided in this section (see p16) to help you accurately plan teaching according to the needs of each child, and to place the children at the appropriate level within *Collins Primary Focus: Spelling*. The words within the diagnostic test should be dictated to the children. It is suggested that at 90% accuracy children should move up to the next level. At less than 20% accuracy children should move to the level below.

Assessment Focuses

Your judgements through formative and summative assessment can be combined to reach a conclusion about the level to which each child is working, following levelling guidelines.

The Assessment Focuses which make up the Assessing Pupils' Progress (APP) guidelines are listed within this section for reference. *Collins Primary Focus: Spelling* could be used primarily to collect evidence for **Writing, Assessment Focus 8: Use correct spelling**. However, many of the activities suggested in the integrated *Pupil Book*, *Practice Book* and *Teacher's Guide* could provide evidence for other Reading, Writing, and Speaking and listening Assessment Focuses.

Class record sheets for the main units and for the Progress Units and Dictation activities are provided so that you can monitor progress. An individual record sheet with space for more detailed notes about each child is also provided. These sheets can be photocopied or printed from the CD-ROM.

Reading Assessment Focuses

AF1	Use a range of strategies, including accurate decoding of text, to read for meaning
AF2	Understand, describe, select or retrieve information, events or ideas from texts and use quotation and reference to text
AF3	Deduce, infer or interpret information, events or ideas from texts
AF4	Identify and comment on the structure and organisation of texts, including grammatical and presentational features at text level
AF5	Explain and comment on writers' uses of language, including grammatical and literary features at word and sentence level
AF6	Identify and comment on writers' purposes and viewpoints and the overall effect of the text on the reader
AF7	Relate texts to their social, cultural and historical contexts and literary traditions

Writing Assessment Focuses

AF1	Write imaginative, interesting and thoughtful texts
AF2	Produce texts which are appropriate to task, reader and purpose
AF3	Organise and present whole texts effectively, sequencing and structuring information, ideas and events
AF4	Construct paragraphs and use cohesion within and between paragraphs
AF5	Vary sentences for clarity, purpose and effect
AF6	Write with technical accuracy of syntax and punctuation in phrases, clauses and sentences
AF7	Select appropriate and effective vocabulary
AF8	Use correct spelling

Speaking and listening Assessment Focuses

AF1	**Talking to others** Talk in purposeful and imaginative ways to explore ideas and feelings, adapting and varying structure and vocabulary according to purpose, listeners, and content
AF2	**Talking with others** Listen and respond to others, including in pairs and groups, shaping meanings through suggestions, comments and questions
AF3	**Talking within role-play and drama** Create and sustain different roles and scenarios, adapting techniques in a range of dramatic activities to explore texts, ideas, and issues
AF4	**Talking about talk** Understand the range and uses of spoken language, commenting on meaning and impact and draw on this when talking to others

Statutory Assessment

Children are currently teacher-assessed in reading, writing and mathematics at the end of Key Stage 1. Test papers can be used to aid the teacher-assessment decision. As part of the writing assessment, children must demonstrate their skills in grammar, spelling, vocabulary and punctuation.

Collins Primary Focus: Spelling supports you to implement a progressive, whole-school approach to developing children's spelling skills. It introduces all the key spelling rules and provides a range of strategies to help children to become confident, accurate spellers.

The Grammar, Punctuation and Spelling Test

Following Lord Bew's independent review of Key Stage 2 assessment, the government has brought in a new statutory English Grammar, Punctuation and Spelling Test for all children in England in Year 6.

The majority of the test content is drawn from En3: Writing at Key Stage 2 (National Curriculum 1999), but some relevant areas of content are included from across the programme of study for English, for example vocabulary (En2: Reading) and Standard English (En1: Speaking and listening).

Children working below level 3 will be exempt from the tests and those working above level 5 can be entered for a separate level 6 test. Children entered for the level 6 test must first complete the levels 3–5 test and demonstrate that they are performing at a good level 5.

The test, for levels 3–5, will consist of two elements:

- a 45-minute short answer paper testing grammar, punctuation and vocabulary
- a 15-minute (although not strictly timed) spelling test.

The leve 6 test then consists of three elements:

- a 30-minute extended writing task
- a 20-minute short answer paper testing grammar, punctuation and vocabulary
- a 10-minute (although not strictly timed) spelling test.

The separate spelling test will require children to apply the correct spelling of a given word, within the context of a sentence. At level 6, this will have the same layout, but will be testing higher-level spellings. The spelling element of the short answer test requires children to apply their knowledge of spelling conventions (as laid out in the National Curriculum) in the context of questions rather than straightforward spelling of words. A typical example of this would be for children to apply their knowledge of prefixes by adding a prefix to a root word to change its meaning. The children therefore need a good understanding of spelling conventions in order to apply these in a range of questions.

Preparing children for the Key Stage 2 test

Collins Primary Focus: Spelling Introductory level introduces children to some of the key language skills that they will need to develop for the end of Key Stage 2 assessment.

The vocabulary that is used throughout the course is in line with the formal terminology used in the test, thus providing the children with asposure to the difficult meta language used within the test. By the time the children take the final test, they will be familiar with the terminology, understand what it means and be able to apply the appropriate skill.

Skills progression across the course

Each unit in the *Collins Primary Focus* series (books Introductory–4) has been clearly mapped to the test codes for the final Year 6 test. This allows you, as teachers, to see the progress that children are making towards attaining each of the skills that will be assessed.

INTRODUCTORY BOOK

Moving from level 2 to 3

Developing knowledge of phonics in spelling and common letter strings.

BOOK 1

Level 3 concepts

Consolidating knowledge of common prefixes and suffixes and use of phonics in spelling.

BOOK 2

Moving from level 3 to 4

Developing a secure knowledge of spelling strategies including use of homophones.

BOOK 3

Level 4 concepts

Consolidating a secure knowledge of prefixes, suffixes, word families, root words to apply to spellings.

BOOK 4

Moving from level 4 to 5

Ability to use a range of strategies to spell unfamiliar words with unstressed vowels and silent letters.

TEST REVISION BOOKS

including level 6

Revision lessons.

In the Introductory Book the children will be consolidating and developing their knowledge of level 2 concepts and skills whilst touching on some level 3 elements. These directly relate to skills that are tested during the GAPS Test at the end of Year 6, including:

- developing knowledge of rules used for pluralisation
- the use of common suffixes and their spellings
- breaking compound words into parts to aid spelling
- the use of common prefixes and their spellings
- developing knowledge of common letter strings and phonemes as an aid to spelling.

Test reference codes

Unit number and name	National Curriculum objectives KEY STAGE 1(WRITING)	Level	Working towards test reference code
1 The alphabet	4a: write each letter of the alphabet.	1	
2 The long vowel sound *a*	4.b: use their knowledge of sound–symbol relationships and phonological patterns [for example, consonant clusters and vowel phonemes].	1	
3 The long vowel sound *o*	4.b: use their knowledge of sound–symbol relationships and phonological patterns [for example, consonant clusters and vowel phonemes].	1	
4 The long vowel sound *e*	4.b: use their knowledge of sound–symbol relationships and phonological patterns [for example, consonant clusters and vowel phonemes].	1	
5 The long vowel sound *u*	4.b: use their knowledge of sound–symbol relationships and phonological patterns [for example, consonant clusters and vowel phonemes].	1	
6 The long vowel sound *i*	4.b: use their knowledge of sound–symbol relationships and phonological patterns [for example, consonant clusters and vowel phonemes].	1	
	Progress Unit 1		
7 *Oo* and *u*	4.c: recognise and use simple spelling patterns.	2	
8 Words with *ar*	4.b: use their knowledge of sound–symbol relationships and phonological patterns [for example, consonant clusters and vowel phonemes]. 4.c: recognise and use simple spelling patterns.	2	
9 *Oi* and *oy*	4.b: use their knowledge of sound–symbol relationships and phonological patterns [for example, consonant clusters and vowel phonemes]. 4.c: recognise and use simple spelling patterns.	2	
10 *Ou* and *ow*	4.b: use their knowledge of sound–symbol relationships and phonological patterns [for example, consonant clusters and vowel phonemes]. 4.c: recognise and use simple spelling patterns.	2	

Unit	Objectives		Code
11 Adding -s	4.b: use their knowledge of sound–symbol relationships and phonological patterns [for example, consonant clusters and vowel phonemes]. 4.f: spell words with common prefixes and inflectional endings.	2	sg/ga7.8 sg/ga7.9
12 Adding -ed and -ing	4.b: use their knowledge of sound–symbol relationships and phonological patterns [for example, consonant clusters and vowel phonemes]. 4.f: spell words with common prefixes and inflectional endings.	2	sg/ga4.1 sg/ga7.8
Progress Unit 2			
13 Or, er, ir, ur, air and ear	4.b: use their knowledge of sound–symbol relationships and phonological patterns [for example, consonant clusters and vowel phonemes]. 4.c: recognise and use simple spelling patterns.	2	
14 Wh, ph and ch	4.b: use their knowledge of sound–symbol relationships and phonological patterns [for example, consonant clusters and vowel phonemes]. 4.c: recognise and use simple spelling patterns.	2	
15 Compound words	4.b: use their knowledge of sound–symbol relationships and phonological patterns [for example, consonant clusters and vowel phonemes]. 4.h: use their knowledge of word families and other words.	2	sg/ga7.6
16 Syllables	READING: 1.d: identify syllables in words.	2	
17 The prefixes un- and dis-	4.b: use their knowledge of sound–symbol relationships and phonological patterns [for example, consonant clusters and vowel phonemes]. 4.f: spell words with common prefixes and inflectional endings.	2	sg/ga7.7
18 Ow and ea	4.b: use their knowledge of sound–symbol relationships and phonological patterns [for example, consonant clusters and vowel phonemes]. 4.d: write common letter strings.	2	
19 The suffixes -ful and -ly	4.b: use their knowledge of sound–symbol relationships and phonological patterns [for example, consonant clusters and vowel phonemes]. 4.f: spell words with common prefixes and inflectional endings.	2	sg/ga7.8
Progress Unit 3			
Spellchecker			

Diagnostic test
Collins Primary Focus: Spelling

Word	Spelling Objective	Introductory Pupil Book Unit	Word	Spelling Objective	Introductory Pupil Book Unit
shame	The long vowel sound *a*	2	lifted	Adding *-ed* and *-ing*	12
train	The long vowel sound *a*	2	pecking	Adding *-ed* and *-ing*	12
play	The long vowel sound *a*	2	staying	Adding *-ed* and *-ing*	12
toast	The long vowel sound *o*	3	short	*Or, er, ir, ur, air* and *ear*	13
stone	The long vowel sound *o*	3	fern	*Or, er, ir, ur, air* and *ear*	13
throw	The long vowel sound *o*	3	first	*Or, er, ir, ur, air* and *ear*	13
dream	The long vowel sound *e*	4	burn	*Or, er, ir, ur, air* and *ear*	13
sleep	The long vowel sound *e*	4	chair	*Or, er, ir, ur, air* and *ear*	13
spoon	The long vowel sound *u*	5	clear	*Or, er, ir, ur, air* and *ear*	13
grew	The long vowel sound *u*	5	whale	*Wh, ph* and *ch*	14
glue	The long vowel sound *u*	5	graph	*Wh, ph* and *ch*	14
flute	The long vowel sound *u*	5	chain	*Wh, ph* and *ch*	14
pie	The long vowel sound *i*	6	handbag	Compound words	15
why	The long vowel sound *i*	6	toothbrush	Compound words	15
slide	The long vowel sound *i*	6	banana	Syllables	16
bright	The long vowel sound *i*	6	rocket	Syllables	16
foot	*Oo* and *u*	7	unsafe	The prefixes *un-* and *dis-*	17
pull	*Oo* and *u*	7	distrust	The prefixes *un-* and *dis-*	17
start	Words with *ar*	8	crowd	*Ow* and *ea*	18
point	*Oi* and *oy*	9	blow	*Ow* and *ea*	18
toy	*Oi* and *oy*	9	pear	*Ow* and *ea*	18
mouth	*Ou* and *ow*	10	bread	*Ow* and *ea*	18
crown	*Ou* and *ow*	10	team	*Ow* and *ea*	18
wheels	Adding *-s*	11	helpful	The suffixes *-ful* and *-ly*	19
owls	Adding *-s*	11	softly	The suffixes *-ful* and *-ly*	19
prams	Adding *-s*	11	safely	The suffixes *-ful* and *-ly*	19
rained	Adding *-ed* and *-ing*	12	useful	The suffixes *-ful* and *-ly*	19

Individual record sheet
Collins Primary Focus: Spelling

Name _____

Book _____ Class _____ Year _____

Unit	Comment	Date
1		
2		
3		
4		
5		
6		
PU1		
7		
8		
9		
10		
11		
12		
PU2		
13		
14		
15		
16		
17		
18		
19		
PU3		
SC		

Yearly class record sheet

Collins Primary Focus: Spelling

Class _____

Session _____

Date	Unit	Pupil Book	Practice Book	Resource Sheet	Dictation	Comment
	1 The alphabet					
	2 The long vowel sound a					
	3 The long vowel sound o					
	4 The long vowel sound e					
	5 The long vowel sound u					
	6 The long vowel sound i					
	7 Oo and u					
	8 Words with ar					
	9 Oi and oy					
	10 Ou and ow					
	11 Adding -s					
	12 Adding -ed and -ing					
	13 Or, er, ir, ur, air and ear					
	14 Wh, ph, and ch					
	15 Compound words					
	16 Syllables					
	17 The prefixes un- and dis-					
	18 Ow and ea					
	19 The suffixes -ful and -ly					

Dictation and Progress Unit record sheet

Collins Primary Focus: Spelling

Book _____

Class _____

Names	Dictation																			Progress Units		
	1	2	3	4	5	6	7	8	9	10	11	12	13	14	15	16	17	18	19	1	2	3

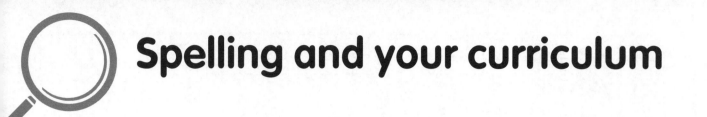

Spelling and your curriculum

Collins Primary Focus: Spelling integrates reading, writing, speaking and listening activities to reinforce spelling rules through every strand of literacy teaching.

Primary National Curriculum

The Primary National Curriculum states that in Key Stage 1 pupils should be taught to:
a) write each letter of the alphabet
b) use their knowledge of sound–symbol relationships and phonological patterns (for example, consonant clusters and vowel phonemes)
c) recognise and use simple spelling patterns
d) write common letter strings
e) spell common words
f) spell words with common prefixes and inflectional endings
g) check the accuracy of their spelling, using word banks and dictionaries
h) use their knowledge of word families and other words
i) identify reasons for misspellings.

See pp18–19 for an overview of how each unit links to the National Curriculum objectives. The learning objective identified for every unit is related to the Primary National Strategy strand six:

- **6: Word structure and spelling.**

Support for Spelling objectives are identified for every unit.

Curriculum for Excellence

All of the units in the *Introductory Pupil Book* relate to this objective from the First level of the Curriculum for Excellence:

Writing: Tools for writing

I can spell the most commonly-used words, using my knowledge of letter patterns and spelling rules and use resource to help me spell tricky or unfamiliar words. LIT 1-21a

National Curriculum for Wales

All of the units in the *Introductory Pupil Book* relate to these objectives from the National Curriculum for Wales Foundation Stage:

Writing: Skills

Children should make progress in their ability to:
- **recognise the alphabetic nature of writing and discriminate between letters**
- **develop their ability to spell common and familiar words in a recognisable way**
- **use a dictionary.**

Revised Northern Ireland Curriculum

All of the units in the *Introductory Pupil Book* relate to these objectives from the Revised Northern Ireland Curriculum Key Stage 1:

Writing:

Pupils should be enabled to:
- use a variety of skills to spell words in their writing
- spell correctly a range of familiar, important and regularly occurring words.

Cambridge International Primary Programme

Collins Primary Focus: Spelling Introductory Pupil Book	Primary English Curriculum Framework Phonics, Spelling and Vocabulary
1 The alphabet	Know the name and most common sound associated with every letter in the English alphabet (Stage 1)
2 The long vowel sound *a*	Learn the different common spellings of long vowel phonemes (Stage 2)
3 The long vowel sound *o*	Learn the different common spellings of long vowel phonemes (Stage 2)
4 The long vowel sound *e*	Learn the different common spellings of long vowel phonemes (Stage 2)
5 The long vowel sound *u*	Learn the different common spellings of long vowel phonemes (Stage 2)
6 The long vowel sound *i*	Learn the different common spellings of long vowel phonemes (Stage 2)
7 *Oo* and *u*	Learn the different common spellings of long vowel phonemes (Stage 2)
8 Words with *ar*	Identify separate sounds (phonemes) within words, which may be represented by more than one letter (Stage 1)
9 *Oi* and *oy*	Learn the different common spellings of long vowel phonemes (Stage 2)
10 *Ou* and *ow*	Learn the different common spellings of long vowel phonemes (Stage 2)
11 Adding *-s*	Recognise common word endings e.g. *-s*, *-ed*, *-ing* (Stage 1)
12 Adding *-ed* and *-ing*	Recognise common word endings e.g. *-s*, *-ed*, *-ing* (Stage 1)
13 *Or, er, ir, ur, air* and *ear*	Identify separate sounds (phonemes) within words, which may be represented by more than one letter (Stage 1)
14 *Wh, ph* and *ch*	Identify separate sounds (phonemes) within words, which may be represented by more than one letter, e.g. 'th', 'ch', 'sh' (Stage 1)
15 Compound words	Identify syllables and split familiar compound words into parts (Stage 2)
16 Syllables	Identify syllables and split familiar compound words into parts (Stage 2)
17 The prefixes *un-* and *dis-*	Spell words with common prefixes and suffixes (e.g. *un-*, *dis-*, *-ful*, *-ly*) (Stage 2)
18 *Ow* and *ea*	Identify separate sounds (phonemes) within words, which may be represented by more than one letter (Stage 1)
19 The suffixes *-ful* and *-ly*	Spell words with common prefixes and suffixes (e.g. *un-*, *dis-*, *-ful*, *-ly*) (Stage 2)

Unit by unit overview chart

	Unit focus	Learning objectives	Support for Spelling	*Collins Primary Literacy links* / *Collins Primary Focus: Grammar and Punctuation* links
1 The alphabet	To secure understanding and use of the terms 'vowel' and 'consonant'	Use phonic knowledge to write simple regular words and make phonetically plausible attempts at more complex words	Y2 Term 1: Children have completed phase 5 of the Phonics programme and are ready to extend their knowledge of the English spelling system	**CPL: Pupil Book 2** Unit 8 From A to Z
2 The long vowel sound *a*	To secure identification, spelling and reading of the long vowel /ai/ in simple words To revise and extend the reading and spelling of words containing different spellings of the long vowel /ai/	Spell new words using phonics as the prime approach Recognise and use alternative ways of spelling the graphemes already taught, for example that the /ae/ sound can be spelled with *ai*, *ay* or *a-e*	Y2 Term 1 (i): To secure the reading and spelling of words containing different spellings for phonemes	**CPL: Big Book 2A** Unit 1 The Twins **CPL: Big Book 2A** Unit 2 Make an Octopus Puppet
3 The long vowel sound *o*	To secure identification, spelling and reading of the long vowel /oa/ in simple words To revise and extend the reading and spelling of words containing different spellings of the long vowel /oa/	Spell new words using phonics as the prime approach Recognise and use alternative ways of spelling the phonemes already taught	Y2 Term 1 (i): To secure the reading and spelling of words containing different spellings for phonemes	**CPL: Big Book 2A** Unit 1 The Twins **CPL: Big Book 2A** Unit 3 Two Feet
4 The long vowel sound *e*	To secure identification, spelling and reading of the long vowel /ee/ in simple words To revise and extend the reading and spelling of words containing different spellings of the long vowel /ee/	Spell new words using phonics as the prime approach Recognise and use alternative ways of spelling the phonemes already taught	Y2 Term 1 (i): To secure the reading and spelling of words containing different spellings for phonemes	**CPL: Big Book 2A** Unit 1 The Twins **CPL: Big Book 2A** Unit 2 Cress Creatures – Woolly Sheep **CPL: Big Book 2A** Unit 3 Street Sounds, Two Feet

Unit	Objective	Objective	Reference
5 The long vowel sound *u*	To secure identification, spelling and reading of the long vowel /(y)oo/ in simple words To revise and extend the reading and spelling of words containing different spellings of the long vowel /(y)oo/	Spell new words using phonics as the prime approach Recognise and use alternative ways of spelling the phonemes already taught	Y2 Term 1 (i): To secure the reading and spelling of words containing different spellings for phonemes	**CPL: Big Book 2A** Unit 1 The Twins
6 The long vowel sound *i*	To secure identification, spelling and reading of the long vowel /igh/ in simple words To revise and extend the reading and spelling of words containing different spellings of the long vowel /igh/	Spell new words using phonics as the prime approach Recognise and use alternative ways of spelling the phonemes already taught	Y2 Term 1 (i): To secure the reading and spelling of words containing different spellings for phonemes	**CPL: Big Book 2A** Unit 1 The Twins **CPL: Big Book 2A** Unit 3 Two Feet
Progress Unit 1	Revision and assessment			
7 Oo and *u*	To identify the common spelling pattern for the short vowel phoneme oo and to spell words with this spelling pattern	Spell new words using phonics as the prime approach	Y2 Term 1 (i): To secure the reading and spelling of words containing different spellings for phonemes	**CPL: Big Book 2C** Unit 10 Morris Plays Hide and Seek **CPL: Big Book 2C** Unit 10 Mountain Mona
8 Words with *ar*	To identify the common spelling pattern for the vowel phoneme ar and to spell words with this spelling pattern	Spell new words using phonics as the prime approach	Y4 Term 2 (i) To investigate and learn to spell words with common letter strings	**CPL: Big Book 2B** Unit 6 Jelly on a Plate

continued overleaf

Unit by unit overview chart *continued*

	Unit focus	Learning objectives	Support for Spelling	Collins Primary Literacy links / Collins Primary Focus: Grammar and Punctuation links
9 Oi and oy	To identify the common spelling pattern for the vowel phoneme *oi* (oi/oy) and to spell words with these spelling pattern	Spell new words using phonics as the prime approach Recognise and use alternative ways of spelling the phonemes already taught	Y4 Term 2 (i): To investigate and learn to spell words with common letter strings	**CPL: Big Book 2A** Unit 3 Funky Feet
10 Ou and ow	To identify the common spelling patterns for the vowel phoneme *ou* and *ow* and to spell words with these spelling patterns	Spell new words using phonics as the prime approach	Y2 Term 1 (i): To secure the reading and spelling of words containing different spellings for phonemes Y4 Term 2 (i): To investigate and learn to spell words with common letter strings	**CPL: Big Book 2C** Unit 10 Morris Plays Hide and Seek **CPL: Big Book 2C** Unit 10 Mountain Mona
11 Adding -s	To use the word ending -s (plural) to support reading and spelling	Spell new words using phonics as the prime approach Use knowledge of common inflections in spelling, such as plurals	Y2 Term 2 (ii): To learn how to add common inflections (suffixes) to words e.g. plurals	**CPL: Big Book 2C** Unit 8 Index of Eggs and Chicks **CPL: Big Book 2C** Unit 8 Using This Dictionary **CPL: Big Book 2C** Unit 9 Two Tongue-twisters **CPF: Grammar and Punctuation Introductory Pupil Book** Unit 12 Singular and plural

Unit	Objective	Spelling	NLS Reference	Resources
12 Adding -ed and -ing	To use the word endings -ed (past) and -ing (present) to support reading and spelling	Spell new words using phonics as the prime approach Use knowledge of common inflections in spelling	Y2 Term 1 (ii): To understand and begin to learn the conventions for adding the suffix -ed for past tense and -ing for present tense	**CPL: Big Book 2B** Unit 7 The Last Noo-Noo **CPL: Big Book 2B** Unit 7 The Worst Witch **CPF: Grammar and Punctuation Introductory Pupil Book** Unit 5 Verbs, Unit 11 Verbs (past tense)
Progress Unit 2	Revision and assessment			
13 Or, er, ir, ur, air and ear	To identify the common spelling patterns for the vowel phonemes or, er, and air and to spell words with these spelling patterns	Spell new words using phonics as the prime approach	Y4 Term 2 (ii): To investigate and learn to spell words with common letter strings	**CPL: Big Book 2A** Unit 1 Class Six and the Very Big Rabbit **CPL: Big Book 2B** Unit 5 Snake Charm
14 Wh, ph and ch	To spell words with the digraphs wh, ph and ch (as in Christopher)	Spell new words using phonics as the prime approach	Y4 Term 2 (i): To investigate and learn to spell words with common letter strings	**CPL: Big Book 2B** Unit 5 Eggs and Chicks **CPL: Big Book 2B** Unit 6 Hot Food
15 Compound words	To split familiar oral and written compound words into their component parts	Spell with increasing accuracy and confidence, drawing on word recognition and knowledge of word structure	Y2 Term 2 (i): To split compound words into their component parts and to use this knowledge to support spelling	**CPL: Big Book 2B** Unit 5 Butterfly Life Cycle

continued overleaf

Unit by unit overview chart continued

	Unit focus	Learning objectives	Support for Spelling	Collins Primary Literacy links / Collins Primary Focus: Grammar and Punctuation links
16 Syllables	To discriminate syllables in spoken multi-syllable words and to discriminate and identify syllables in written words	Read and spell phonically decodable two syllable and three syllable words	Y2 Term 3 (ii): To discriminate syllables in multisyllabic words as an aid to spelling	**CPL: Big Book 2B** Unit 5 Butterfly Life Cycle **CPL: Big Book 2B** Unit 6 Spaghetti! Spaghetti!
17 The prefixes un- and dis-	To spell words with common prefixes such as un- and dis- to indicate the negative	Spell new words using phonics as the prime approach	Y2 Term 3 (i): To add common prefixes to root words and to understand how they change meaning	**CPL: Big Book 2C** Unit 4 A Kiss from a Princess **CPL: Big Book 2C** Unit 4 The Frog Prince
18 Ow and ea	To investigate words which have the same spelling patterns but different sounds	Spell new words using phonics as the prime approach	Y4 Term 2 (i): To investigate and learn to spell words with common letter strings	**CPL: Big Book 2C** Unit 9 Two Tongue-twisters **CPL: Big Book 2C** Unit 9 Riddles
19 The suffixes -ful and -ly	To spell words with the common suffixes -ful and -ly	Use knowledge of common inflections in spelling	Y2 Term 2 (ii): To learn how to add common suffixes to words	**CPL: Big Book 2B** Unit 7 Jill Murphy
Progress Unit 3	Revision and assessment			
Spellchecker	Identifying and correcting misspelled words			

Unit by unit teaching notes

The alphabet

Planning

- **Unit focus**

  To secure understanding and use of the terms 'vowel' and 'consonant'

- **Learning objective**

  Use phonic knowledge to write simple regular words and make phonetically plausible attempts at more complex words

- **Support for Spelling**

  Y2 Term 1: Children have completed phase 5 of the Phonics programme and are ready to extend their knowledge cf the English spelling system

  CPL: Pupil Book 2 Unit 8 From A to Z

Introduction

Overview

This unit builds upon and consolidates a programme of discrete phonic teaching.

By the end of the unit, the children should be secure in their knowledge and understanding of the letters of the alphabet.

Rule

There are 26 letters in the alphabet.

There are five vowels: a, e, i, o, u.

The other letters are called consonants.

All words have a vowel or the letter *y* in them.

Revisit–Explain–Use

- Display an alphabet frieze or write the letters of the alphabet on the board.

- Elicit from the children:
  - the letters are called the alphabet
  - there are 26 letters in the alphabet
  - there are two types of letters – vowels and consonants
  - there are five vowels, a, e, i, o, u – 'Angry elephants in orange underwear' is a mnemonic that will help the children to remember this.

- Encourage the children to open the fingers of one hand and point to each finger in turn as they say 'Angry elephants in orange underwear' or 'a, e, i, o, u'. It is vital that the children are confident in using the name of a letter and the sound (phoneme) that a letter represents.

Teach–Model–Define

- Tell the children that all words must have at least one vowel or the letter *y* in them.

- Write examples of both on the board.

  Examples

dog	bed	bus	sock	cry	rang
flag	fly	cat	my	list	log

  Invite the children to name and underline the vowel or letter 'y' in each word.

- Practise auditory discrimination of vowel sounds. This can be difficult for some of the children and ongoing practice should be given as appropriate. Distribute [a] [e] [i] [o] [u] 'show me' cards and invite the children to hold up the appropriate card, showing the vowel heard in words that you say aloud.

  Examples

fish	left	bag	cot	sun	pin
red	bus	loft	flat	mad	flip
rush	pram	smell	rock		

- Write words on the board and give practice in changing the vowel to make new words.

  Examples

bed	cat	him	lock	fin	sink
bid	cut	ham	lick	fan	sank
bad	cot	hum	luck	fun	sunk

- Write words on the board and give practice in changing the first consonant (onset) to make new words.

  Examples

fan	men	cot
man	Ben	dot
can	den	got
ran	hen	hot
ban	Jen	jot
Jan	pen	lot
pan	ten	pot
tan		rot

- Now try changing the final consonant to make new words.

Practise–Explore–Investigate

- Distribute magnetic letters and boards. Ask the children to change one letter at a time – first, middle, last to make a new word, for example, change the *h* in hat to a *p*. What word do you get? Change the *a* in pat to an *e*. What word do you get?

- Challenge the children to make as many changes to a word as they can by changing one letter at a time.

  Example:
  hat → pat → pet → pen → pin → fin → fan

Introductory Pupil Book

pages 4–5

Resource Sheet 1

Enrichment

- Look at words ending in -*ss*, -*ff* and -*ll* with short vowels. Write some examples on the board and ask the children to suggest more.

  Examples

hiss	fuss	cuff	pill	bell
kiss	lass	huff	till	fell
miss	pass	muff	will	sell
mess	mass	puff	hill	tell
less			fill	well

- Ask the children to read aloud:

  'Ding, dong, dell,
  Pussy in the well'

  What do they notice about the words 'dell' and 'well'? The children should come to the conclusion that the double letter at the end of each word only makes one sound.

  Ask the children to use onset and rime to write other new words with this pattern.

  Ask the children to change the vowel sound in well. Change the *e* to *i* to make a new word, will.

- Ask the children to change the vowel to make other words with this pattern, for example:
  bell → bill
  fell → fill
  tell → till.

- Ask the children to scan a piece of text to find words which have different double letters at the end, for example, *The Three Little Pigs*: huff, puff.

- A useful mnemonic to help children remember the double letters at the end of words is: 'Silly foolish letters, they don't stand on their own' for example, ss, ff, ll.

Apply–Assess–Reflect AfL

- Give the children the opportunity to reflect on their learning.

- Elicit the key points
  - the alphabet has 26 letters, 21 consonants and five vowels.

- Ask the children to write:
  - the five vowels
  - five consonants
  - five words, each word with a different vowel.

Dictation

1. The fat dog sat on the big rug.
2. The fox ran in the mud.
3. The pan, jug, pot and lid are wet.
4. The duck swam in the pond.
5. I lost the plug for the sink.

Word Book

- Encourage the children to add new or challenging words to *My Third Word Book*.

Answers

Introductory Pupil Book

pages 4–5

Getting started

Write a word to name each picture. Underline the vowel in each word.

1. c<u>u</u>p
2. d<u>o</u>g
3. b<u>e</u>d
4. b<u>i</u>n
5. v<u>a</u>n
6. s<u>o</u>ck
7. r<u>i</u>ng
8. f<u>i</u>sh
9. c<u>u</u>ff

More to think about

Change the vowel to make new words.

1. hat → hut → hot

Possible answers:

2. pen → *pan* → *pin*
3. fin → *fan* → *fun*
4. sick → *sack* → *sock*
5. lift → *left* → *loft*
6. flip → *flap* → *flop*

Now try these

Change the first consonant to make two more rhyming words each time. The first one has been done to help you.

1. pan → can → man

Possible answers:

2. run: *bun, fun, gun, nun*
3. jet: *bet, get, pet, wet*

4. dog: *bog, cog, hog, jog, log*
5. lip: *dip, hip, pip, sip, tip*
6. wag: *bag, hag, nag, sag, rag*
7. men: *Ben, den, hen, pen, ten*
8. pit: *bit, hit, lit, sit, fit*
9. hut: *but, cut, jut, nut, rut*
10. hot: *cot, dot, lot, not, pot*

Resource Sheet 1

A

ⓐ b c d ⓔ f g h ⓘ j k l m
n ⓞ p q r s t ⓤ v w x y z

B

Possible answers:

1. cat cut cot
2. not *nut net*
3. beg *bag big bug*
4. jug *jig jag jog*
5. fin *fan fun*

C

Possible answers:

1. ham hat had has
2. hip *hid him hit his*
3. wed *web wet*
4. rot *rob rod*

Unit 2

The long vowel sound *a*

Planning

- **Unit focus**

  To secure identification, spelling and reading of the long vowel /ai/ in simple words

  To revise and extend the reading and spelling of words containing different spellings of the long vowel /ai/

- **Learning objectives**

  Spell new words using phonics as the prime approach

  Recognise and use alternative ways of spelling the graphemes already taught, for example that the /ae/ sound can be spelled with *ai*, *ay* or *a-e*

- **Support for Spelling**

  Y2 Term 1 (i): To secure the reading and spelling of words containing different spellings for phonemes

  CPL: **Big Book 2A Unit 1** The Twins
  CPL: **Big Book 2A Unit 2** Make an Octopus Puppet

Introduction

Overview

This unit builds upon and consolidates a programme of discrete phonic teaching.

By the end of the unit, the children should be secure in their knowledge and understanding of the alternative spellings for the long vowel sound /ai/.

Rule

The long vowel sound /ai/ can be spelled in different ways:

a-e as in cake

ai as in rain

ay as in play.

Revisit–Explain–Use

- Revise the vowels – their names and their short vowel sounds.

- Invite the children to recite the mnemonic, 'Angry elephants in orange underwear', the names of the letters (A, E, I, O, U) and the sounds of the letters (*a, e, i, o, u*) in chronological order.

- Practise auditory discrimination. Play 'Can you hear the name or the sound of a letter in words?' Say words with the short *a* sound and words with the long /ai/ sound. The children answer 'sound' or 'name'.

  Examples

hat	tray	pain	train
cake	sand	bag	wag

- Explain to the children that when they hear the sound of the letter it is a short vowel sound and when they hear the name of the letter it is a long vowel sound. It is very important for later spelling that the children know the difference between a short vowel and a long vowel.

- Practise auditory discrimination. Play 'Can you hear a short vowel sound or a long vowel sound in words?'

  Examples

pan	rain	play	rat
late	plane	man	jag

Teach–Model–Define

Word list 2

- Explain to the children that the short vowel sound is written *a*, for example, tap, rag.

- Explain how the long vowel sound is written in words like rain, plate and tray, that is, *ai*, *a-e* and *ay*. (*ei*, as in weigh and *ea* as in great should be looked at in 'Enrichment' work.)

- Write the following words on the board and help the children to see when the different long /ai/ sounds are used: play, chain, day, tray, paint, hail, clay.

  Note: ai is usually found in the middle of words; ay is usually found at the end of words with one syllable.

- Give practice in identifying whether the long /ai/ sound is heard in the middle or at the end of words. Ask the children to respond 'middle' or 'end' to words that you say aloud.

  Examples
  tray   chain   hay
  clay   pain   stain

- Give practice in showing the written representation of the sound heard. Ask the children to hold up the correct card [ai] or [ay] to represent the sound heard in words like play and paint. Whiteboards could be used instead.

- Write rake, game, cave and plate on the board and help the children to see when the (a-e) representation is used, that is, with the letters *k*, *m*, *v* and *t*.

- Give practice in writing words with the long /ai/ sound. Using individual whiteboards and pens, ask the children to write words in groups that you dictate. This will reinforce letter sequence and motor memory.

- Encourage the children to apply their knowledge of the different representations of the long /ai/ sound when spelling.

Practise–Explore–Investigate

- Give the children a selection of words with the long vowel sound /ai/ represented in different ways. Ask the children to sort words into groups – those with *ai*, those with *ay* and those with *a-e*.

- Challenge the children to make lists of words which have the different representations of the long /ai/ sound. Encourage the use of onset and rime as a spelling strategy

ai	*ay*	*a-e*
train	hay	tame
stain	say	name
nail		cake
pail		make
		date
		plate

- Ask the children to exchange their lists with a partner and discuss any misspelled words to arrive at the correct spelling. Encourage children to refer back to the rule.

Introductory Pupil Book

pages 6–7

Introductory Practice Book

page 3

Resource Sheet 2

A

B

Enrichment

- Investigate other representations of the long vowel sound /ai/, such as *ea*, as in great and break; *ei* as in neighbour and weigh. As a starting point, look at a number of cereal packets with the word 'Breakfast' written on them and invite the children to comment on the sound made by the *ea* letter string. It is a single sound.

  Ask the children what they notice about the word 'cereal'? It has the letters *ea* in it but both vowels are pronounced. Ask the children to design a packet for a new breakfast cereal.

- Similarly, look at a piece of maths text where the word 'weigh' is used. Ask the children what they notice about the word 'weigh'. It contains another letter pattern (*ei*) that makes the long vowel sound /ai/.

Apply–Assess–Reflect AfL

- Give the children opportunity to reflect on their learning.
- Elicit the key points:
  - the difference between short and long vowels (encourage the children to give examples)
  - the different ways to write the long vowel /ai/ in words (encourage the children to give examples).
- Ask the children to write two examples of words with each letter pattern *ai*, *ay*, *a-e* and to underline the vowel phoneme (long vowel sound).

Dictation

1. I left my case on the train.
2. We paid for the rake and the spade.
3. I can play the game with you.
4. The snail made a trail on the path.
5. The cake is on a plate on the tray.

Word Book WB

- Encourage the children to add new or challenging words to *My Third Word Book*.

Answers

Introductory Pupil Book

pages 6–7

Getting started

Write a word to name each picture. Circle the letters that make the long *a* sound.

1. c(a)k(e)
2. c(a)s(e)
3. wh(a)l(e)
4. gr(a)p(e)s
5. r(a)k(e)
6. c(a)v(e)
7. g(a)t(e)
8. sp(a)d(e)
9. pl(a)t(e)

More to think about

1. Write a word to name each picture. Circle the letters that make the long *a* sound.

   a) r(ai)n
   b) ch(ai)n
   c) p(ai)nt
   d) sn(ai)l
   e) tr(ai)n
   f) s(ai)l

2. Use the clues to work out the *ai* words.

   a) a path or marks you can follow *trail*
   b) drops of hard, icy rain *hail*
   c) what a dog wags *tail*

Now try these

1. Write the rhyming words in a list.
   Say, stay, away, play

2. Add more words that end with *-ay* to your list.
   Possible additional words:
   bay, day, gay, hay, lay, may, tray

3. Write a short rhyme using words from your list.
   (Children's own answers.)

Introductory Practice Book

page 3

A *ai*, *ay*, *a-e*, examples: *train, day, make*

B 1. rain   2. *game*   3. *case*
   4. *snail*   5. *cake*   6. *grape*

Resource Sheet 2

A 1. tr(ay)   2. c(a)k(e)   3. tr(ai)n
   4. sk(a)t(e)   5. sn(ai)l   6. ch(ai)n
   7. h(ay)   8. pr(ay)   9. s(a)f(e)

B *Possible answers:*

wake	pain	may	
cake	train	bay	say
bake	gain	day	clay
fake	main	gay	fray
lake	rain	hay	sway
make	stain	lay	play
rake	vain	pay	stay
take	brain	ray	
flake	drain	way	

Unit 3

The long vowel sound *o*

Planning

- **Unit focus**

  To secure identification, spelling and reading of the long vowel /oa/ in simple words

  To revise and extend the reading and spelling of words containing different spellings of the long vowel /oa/

- **Learning objectives**

  Spell new words using phonics as the prime approach

  Recognise and use alternative ways of spelling the phonemes already taught

- **Support for Spelling**

  Y2 Term 1(i): To secure the reading and spelling of words containing different spellings for phonemes

  CPL: Big Book 2A Unit 1 The Twins
  CPL: Big Book 2A Unit 3 Two Feet

Introduction

Overview

This unit builds upon and consolidates a programme of discrete phonic teaching.

By the end of the unit, children should be secure in their knowledge and understanding of the alternative spellings for the long vowel sound /oa/.

Rule

The long vowel sound /oa/ can be spelled in different ways:

oa as in coat

ow as in crow

o-e as in rose.

Revisit–Explain–Use

- Revise the vowels – their names and their short vowel sounds.

- Invite the children to recite the mnemonic, 'Angry elephants in orange underwear', the names of letters (A, E, I, O, U) and the sounds of the letters (*a, e, i, o, u*) in chronological order.

- Practise auditory discrimination. Play 'Can you hear the name or the sound of a letter in words?' Say words with the short *o* sound and words with the long /oa/ sound. Children answer 'sound' or 'name'.

  Examples

  | hot | coat | row | slow |
  | hope | loft | dot | dog |

Note: Remind the children that when they hear the sound of the letter it is a short vowel sound and when they hear the name of the letter it is a long vowel sound. It is very important for later spelling that the children know the difference between a short vowel and a long vowel.

- Practise auditory discrimination. Play 'Can you hear a short vowel sound or a long vowel sound in words?'

  Examples

boat	foal	blow	soap
grow	mow	road	show
pot	rod	shop	cost

Teach–Model–Define

- Explain to the children that the short vowel sound is written *o*, for example, top, dog.

- Explain how the long vowel sound is written in words like road, home and slow, that is, *oa*, *o-e* and *ow*. (*oe* as in toe and *o* as in go should be looked at in 'Enrichment' work.)

- Write the following words on the board and investigate with the children when to use the different representations of the long /oa/ sound: show, boat, snow, flow, float, foam, mow. Ask the children to look at the words and to read them. Can they put the words into two lists? What do they notice about the words in the two different lists?

  Note: *oa is usually found in the middle of words. ow is usually found at the end of words with one syllable.*

- Practise auditory discrimination. Give practice in identifying whether the long /oa/ sound is heard in the middle or at the end of words. Ask the children to respond 'middle' or 'end' to words you say aloud.

  Examples
toast	goal	grow
throw	toad	low

- Give children practice in showing the written representation of the sound they hear. Ask them to hold up the correct card [*oa*] or [*ow*] which represents the sound heard in words like goal and grow. Whiteboards could be used.

- Write joke, bone and nose on the board and investigate with the children when the *o-e* representation is used (with the letters *k*, *n* and *s*).

- Give practice in writing words with the long /oa/ sound. Using individual whiteboards and pens, ask the children to write words in groups that you dictate. This will reinforce letter sequence and motor memory.

- Encourage the children to apply their knowledge about the different representations of the long /oa/ sound when spelling.

Practise–Explore–Investigate

- Give out cards with words containing the focus phoneme /oa/. Use the **Word list** for examples. Ask the children to read a word and find others with the same spelling of the long vowel sound. When sorted into groups, each child should take a turn to read their words aloud. Encourage speed and accuracy.

- Challenge the children to make lists of words which have the different representation of the long *o* sound. Encourage the use of onset and rime as a spelling strategy.

  Examples

oa	ow	o-e
coat	show	hole
boat	blow	pole
coast		
toast		

- Ask the children to exchange their lists with a partner and discuss any misspelled words to arrive at the correct spelling. Encourage children to refer back to the rule.

Introductory Pupil Book

pages 8–9

Introductory Practice Book

page 4

Resource Sheet 3

A

B

Enrichment

- Investigate other representations of the long vowel sound /oa/, such as *o* in go and so; *oe* in toe, hoe, doe, foe and Joe. Ask the children to think of other words that rime with Joe. Remind the children that changing the onset will help.

- Ask the children to look at column 2 of 'The first 100 high-frequency words' (see p124) and to highlight three words with the /oa/ sound.

Apply–Assess–Reflect AfL

- Give the children the opportunity to reflect on their learning.
- Elicit the key points:
  - the difference between short and long vowels, o/oa (encourage the children to give examples)
  - the different ways to write the long vowel /oa/ in words (encourage the children to give examples).
- Ask the children to write two examples of words with each letter pattern oa, ow, o-e and to underline the vowel phoneme (long vowel sound).

Dictation

1. There is a lot of snow on the road.
2. I hope he can row the boat.
3. My coat has a bow on it.
4. We need a long rope to tow the bus.
5. The coach drove us to the coast.

Word Book

- Encourage the children to add new or challenging words to *My Third Word Book*.

Answers

Introductory Pupil Book

pages 8–9

Getting started

Write an *oa* word to name each picture. Circle the letters that make the long o sound.

1. b(oa)t
2. f(oa)l
3. r(oa)d
4. t(oa)st
5. s(oa)p
6. cl(oa)k
7. g(oa)l
8. g(oa)t
9. c(oa)ch

More to think about

1. Change the first letter to make a rhyming word. Circle the letters that make the long o sound.

   a) c(o)n(e) → b(o)n(e)

   Possible answers:

   b) h(o)p(e) → sl(o)p(e) → r(o)p(e)

   c) r(o)d(e) → c(o)d(e) → str(o)d(e)

2. Change the first letter to make at least three more rhyming words each time. The first one has been done to help you.

   a) m(o)l(e) → p(o)l(e) → v(o)l(e) → h(o)l(e)

   Possible answers:

   b) p(o)k(e) → j(o)k(e) → w(o)k(e) → c(o)k(e)

   c) h(o)s(e) → n(o)s(e) → r(o)s(e) → p(o)s(e)

Now try these

1. a) Write the rhyming words in a list.
      know, crow, snow, bow
   b) Add more *ow* words to your list.
      Possible additions: glow, low, mow, slow, throw
   c) Write a short rhyme using words from your list.
      (Children's own answers.)

2. Write at least three more words for each different way the long o sound can be written.

oa	o-e	ow
throat	cone	flow
road	bone	glow
moan	hose	row
roast	hole	show
toad	stone	blow

Introductory Practice Book

page 4

mole, grow, row, yellow, soap, oat, float, woke,
spoke, poke, groan, stone, tone, flow, low, coat,
window

Resource Sheet 3

A 1. bl(ow)   2. r(o)s(e)   3. c(oa)t

   4. b(ow)   5. t(oa)d   6. sn(ow)

   7. b(o)n(e)   8. p(o)l(e)   9. r(oa)d

B *Possible answers:*

float	mole	crow
boat	hole	bow
oat	pole	blow
coat	sole	snow
goat	stole	flow
moat		grow
stoat		throw

The long vowel sound e

Planning

- **Unit focus**

  To secure identification, spelling and reading of the long vowel /ee/ in simple words

  To revise and extend the reading and spelling of words containing different spellings of the long vowel /ee/

- **Learning objectives**

  Spell new words using phonics as the prime approach

  Recognise and use alternative ways of spelling the phonemes already taught

- **Support for Spelling**

  Y2 Term 1(i): To secure the reading and spelling of words containing different spellings for phonemes

  CPL: Big Book 2A Unit 1 The Twins
  CPL: Big Book 2A Unit 2 Cress Creatures – Woolly Sheep
  CPL: Big Book 2A Unit 3 Street Sounds, Two Feet

Introduction

Overview

This unit builds upon and consolidates a programme of discrete phonic teaching.

By the end of the unit, children should be secure in their knowledge and understanding of the alternative spellings for the long vowel sound /ee/.

Rule

The long vowel sound /ee/ can be spelled in different ways:

ea as in seat

ee as in feet.

Revisit–Explain–Use

- Revise the vowels – their names and their short vowel sounds.

- Invite the children to recite the mnemonic, 'Angry elephants in orange underwear', the names of letters (A, E, I, O, U) and the sounds of the letters (*a, e, i, o, u*) in chronological order.

- Practise auditory discrimination. Play 'Can you hear the name or the sound of a letter in words?' Say words with the short *e* sound and words with the long /ee/ sound. The children answer 'sound' or 'name'.

  Examples
bed	feel	sweet	pet
bead	bell	ten	keep

- Repeat the activity, using the terms 'short vowel' and 'long vowel' and encouraging the children to use them.

  Examples
pen	teeth	vest	read
team	leg	peel	get

Teach–Model–Define

- Explain to the children that the short vowel sound is written e, for example, get, red.

- Explain how the long vowel sound is written in words like feet and read, that is, *ee* and *ea*. (e as in he, be, we, me, she should be looked at in 'Enrichment' work.)

- Some words with *ee* and *ea* are homophones, for example, see and sea. Write the following on the board:

      I can see the book.
      I can swim in the sea.

  Discuss how important it is to use the correct spelling in these sentences. The wrong choice of spelling will change the meaning of the sentences.

- Investigate other common homophones with *ee* and *ea*. Have pairs of words illustrated:

      pair/pear
      week/weak
      tee/tea
      beech/beach

  Invite the children to match illustrated cards into pairs according to the words that sound the same. Ask the children to work out which words have *ee* and which words have *ea*.

Encourage the children to use previous knowledge. Have they seen any of the words written in context, for example, 'week' on the days of the week chart and 'beach' in the non-fiction section in the library?

Other examples:

peel/peal	steel/steal
meet/meat	reed/read
been/bean	reel/real
seem/seam	

- Give practice in writing words with the long /ee/ sound. Using individual whiteboards and pens, ask the children to write words in groups that you dictate. This will reinforce letter sequence and motor memory.

Notes: *Children need a lot of exposure to seeing these words in context as it can be difficult to know which representation of the long /ee/ sound to use. There are no guidelines as to which to use. Almost all long /ee/ words are spelt ee or ea. Words must be learned and children encouraged to use dictionaries. Children with poor visual memories will need extra support and practice in order to commit words to memory successfully.*

Practise–Explore–Investigate

- In small groups or pairs, encourage the children to devise mnemonics which might help them to remember which letters *ee* or *ea* to use. The mnemonics that help children best are often the ones they think of themselves.

  Examples:
  to see – think of two eyes *ee*
  teach – a teacher teaches us to a*dd*

  Note: *This type of activity raises the children's awareness of the fact that it can be difficult to know whether to use ee or ea. A dictionary could be used to check spelling.*

- Challenge children to make lists of words which have the different representations of the long /ee/ sound, *ee* and *ea*.

- Ask the children to exchange their lists with a partner and discuss any misspelled words to arrive at the correct spelling.

Introductory Pupil Book

pages 10–11

Introductory Practice Book

page 5

Resource Sheet 4

A

B

Enrichment

Investigate other representations of the long vowel sound /ee/, such as e in me, be, we, he, she; e-e in eve and Steve; and ey in key. Using 'The first 100 high-frequency words' (see p124), ask the children to find and highlight words with the long vowel sound /ee/ written in a different way, for example, me, be, we, he, she.

Note: *As these words are spread over three columns (75 words), it would be best to select a group of words to include the five identified words.*

Apply–Assess–Reflect AfL

- Give the children the opportunity to reflect on their learning.
- Elicit the key points:
  - the difference between the short and long vowels *e* and *ee* (encourage the children to give examples)
  - the different ways to write the long vowel /ee/ in words (encourage the children to give examples).
- Ask the children to write two examples of words with each letter pattern *ee* and *ea* and to underline the vowel phoneme (long vowel sound).

Dictation

1. I went to meet him from the train.
2. We had three cream cakes.
3. Dad put clean sheets on the bed.
4. The team sat on the green seats.
5. She ate a ripe peach and a bunch of grapes.

Word Book

- Encourage the children to add new or challenging words to *My Third Word Book*.

Answers

Introductory Pupil Book

pages 10–11

Getting started

Write an *ea* word to name each picture. Circle the letters that make the long *e* sound.

1. b(ea)ch
2. b(ea)ds
3. p(ea)ch
4. s(ea)l
5. m(ea)t
6. l(ea)d
7. t(ea)m
8. (ea)st
9. dr(ea)m

More to think about

Add letters to make words.

Possible answers:

1. sheep, *keep, weep, sleep*
2. *feel, heel, peel, wheel*
3. *meet, feet, sleet, sweet*
4. *need, weed, speed, greed*
5. *seek, week, peek, cheek*
6. *see, bee, three, free*

Now try these

Choose the correct words to complete these sentences.

1. Annie likes to splash in the sea.
2. I have *been* to London to *see* the queen.
3. There are seven days in a *week*.
4. Hassan likes to *read* books.
5. I went to *meet* my friend.

Introductory Practice Book

page 5

A Examples: *keep, treat*

B 1. read   2. *sweet*   3. *leaf*
   4. *week*   5. *bean*   6. *wheel*

Resource Sheet 4

A 1. l(ee)k   2. f(ee)d   3. sl(ee)p
   4. p(ea)ch   5. p(ee)l   6. s(ea)l
   7. l(ea)d   8. sw(ee)t   9. t(ea)m

B *Possible answers:*

deep	heat
sleep	cheat
creep	beat
jeep	feat
keep	meat
peep	neat
seep	peat
weep	seat
steep	treat
	wheat

44

Unit 5

The long vowel sound *u*

Planning

- **Unit focus**

  To secure identification, spelling and reading of the long vowel /(y)oo/ in simple words

  To revise and extend the reading and spelling of words containing different spellings of the long vowel /(y)oo/

- **Learning objectives**

  Spell new words using phonics as the prime approach

  Recognise and use alternative ways of spelling the phonemes already taught

- **Support for Spelling**

  Y2 Term 1(i): To secure the reading and spelling of words containing different spellings for phonemes

> **CPL: Big Book 2A** Unit 1 The Twins

Introduction

Overview

This unit builds upon and consolidates a programme of discrete phonic teaching.

By the end of the unit, the children should be secure in their knowledge and understanding of the alternative spellings for the long vowel sound /(y)oo/

Rule

The long vowel sound /(y)oo/ can be spelled in different ways:

oo as in moon

ew as in flew

ue as in clue

u-e as in tune.

Revisit–Explain–Use

- Revise the vowels – their names and their short vowel sounds.

- Invite the children to recite the mnemonic, 'Angry elephants in orange underwear', the names of letters (A, E, I, O, U) and the sounds of the letters (*a, e, i, o, u*) in chronological order.

- Practise auditory discrimination. Play 'Can you hear the name or the sound of a letter in words?' Say words with the short *u* sound and words with the long /(y)oo/ sound. The children answer 'sound' or 'name'.

  Examples

bus	true	fun	room
rude	flute	sun	blue
stew	hut	grew	fuss

- Repeat the activity, using the terms 'short vowel' and 'long vowel'.

  Examples

cut	glue	moon	run
rule	drew	clue	bun

Teach–Model–Define

Word list 5

- Explain to the children that the short vowel sound is written *u*, for example, but, cup.

- Explain how the long vowel sound is written in words like grew, tube, blue and moon, that is, *ew*, *u-e*, *ue* and *oo*.

- Write the following words on the board and investigate with children when to use the different representations of the long /(y)oo/ sound: grew, cool, stew, flew, boot, few, new. Ask the children to look at the words and to read them. Ask the children to put the words into two lists. What do they notice about the words in the two different lists?

  Note: oo is usually found in the middle of words. ew is usually found at the end of words with one syllable.

- Practise auditory discrimination. Give practice in identifying whether the long /(y)oo/ sound is heard in the middle or at the end of words. The children should respond 'middle' or 'end' to words you say aloud.

  Examples
grew	zoom	hoop	flew
room	spoon	crew	drew

- Distribute [oo] and [ew] 'show me' cards and invite children to hold up the card that represents the correct sound in words that you say aloud. Alternatively whiteboards or blank pieces of paper can be used – and the children can write *oo* or *ew*.

  Notes: *There are some exceptions to* ew *at the end of words, for example, blue, true, glue, clue, due and Sue. These words should be directly taught and learned.*

  u-e *is another less common representation of the long vowel /(y)oo/. The following words should be learned: cube, tube, mule, rule, use, fuse, June, tune, prune, cute, flute, jute.*

- Give children practice in writing words with the long /(y)oo/ sound.

- Encourage children to apply their knowledge about the different representations of the long /(y)oo/ sound when spelling.

Practise–Explore–Investigate

- Distribute *oo*, *ew*, *u-e* and *ue* phoneme cards. Say examples of words with the long /(y)oo/ sound represented by *oo*, *ew*, *u-e* and *ue*. Ask the children to hold up the phoneme card that represents the long /(y)oo/ sound in the word they hear.

- Challenge the children to make lists of words which have the different representations of the long /(y)oo/ sound, *oo*, *ew*, *u-e*, *ue*.

- Ask the children to exchange their list with a partner and discuss any misspelled words to arrive at the correct spelling. Encourage the children to refer back to the rule.

Introductory Pupil Book

pages 12–13

Introductory Practice Book

page 6

Resource Sheet 5

Enrichment

- Investigate the *ui* representation in words like fruit, suit, juice, bruise, cruise. Look at a school lunch menu which includes the words 'fruit' and 'juice' and ask the children what they notice – the /(y)oo/ sound is represented by the letters *ui*. Ask the children to read out some sentences you have prepared with the words suit, bruise, and cruise in them. Ask the children to identify the words with the /(y)oo/ sound (suit, bruise, cruise).

- Establish that the /(y)oo/ sound can be represented by the letters *ui*. Ask the children to design a lunch menu that includes the words 'fruit' and 'juice'.

Apply–Assess–Reflect AfL

- Give the children opportunity to reflect on their learning.
- Elicit the key points:
  - the differences between the short and long vowels [u, (y)oo] (encourage the children to give examples)
  - the different ways to write the long vowel /(y)oo/ in words (encourage the children to give examples).
- Ask the children to write two examples of words with each letter pattern *oo*, *ew*, *ue*, *u-e* and to underline the vowel phoneme (long vowel sound).

Dictation

1. The long spoon is in the pot of stew.
2. He threw the tube in the bin.
3. She needs glue and a screw to fix the stool.
4. She can play a tune on the flute.
5. The room has blue paint on the walls.

Word Book WB

- Encourage the children to add new or challenging words to *My Third Word Book*.

Answers

Introductory Pupil Book

pages 12–13

Getting started

Write a word to name each picture. Circle the letters that make the long *u* sound.

1. m(oo)n   2. scr(ew)   3. gl(ue)
4. br(oo)m   5. fl(u)t(e)   6. bl(ue)

More to think about

Write the words from the box with the long *u* sound. One has been done to help you.

grew, *root, true, shoot, mood, threw, cute, tube, fuse*

Now try these

Use the clues to work out the words.

1. a thin, pointed piece of metal used for fixing things together
   screw
2. something that helps to solve a problem
   clue
3. 12 o'clock in the middle of the day
   noon
4. almost cold
   cool
5. a solid shape with six square faces all the same size
   cube

Introductory Practice Book

page 6

A 1. *statue*   2. *rescue*
   3. *continue*   4. *queue*

B *Tuesday*

Resource Sheet 5

A and **B**

spelled *ue*	**spelled *oo***
blue	*food*
glue	*hoot*
true	*root*
clue	*hoof*

spelled *ew*	**spelled *u-e***
drew	*mule*
crew	*fume*
new	*prune*
few	*tune*

The long vowel sound *i*

Planning

- **Unit focus**

  To secure identification, spelling and reading of the long vowel /igh/ in simple words

  To revise and extend the reading and spelling of words containing different spellings of the long vowel /igh/

- **Learning objectives**

  Spell new words using phonics as the prime approach

  Recognise and use alternative ways of spelling the phonemes already taught

- **Support for Spelling**

  Y2 Term 1 (i): To secure the reading and spelling of words containing different spellings for phonemes

  CPL: **Big Book 2A** Unit 1 The Twins
  CPL: **Big Book 2A** Unit 3 Two Feet

Introduction

Overview

This unit builds upon and consolidates a programme of discrete phonic teaching.

By the end of the unit, the children should be secure in their knowledge and understanding of the alternative spellings for the long vowel sound /igh/.

Rule

The long vowel sound /igh/ can be spelled in different ways:

ie as in lie

igh as in night

i-e as in bike

y as in cry.

Revisit–Explain–Use

- Revise the vowels – their names and their short vowel sounds.

- Invite the children to recite the mnemonic, 'Angry elephants in orange underwear', the names of the letters (A, E, I, O, U) and the sounds of the letters (*a, e, i, o, u*) in chronological order.

- Practise auditory discrimination. Play 'Can you hear the name or the sound of a letter in words?' Say words with the short *i* sound and words with the long /igh/ sound. The children should answer 'sound' or 'name'.

  Examples

fin	might	ripe	pit
fine	fry	white	tie
sick	fight	shy	bin

- Repeat the activity, using the terms 'short vowel' and 'long vowel'.

  Examples

tin	light	pipe	sit
why	lit	mine	pie

Teach–Model–Define

- Explain to the children that the short vowel sound is written *i*, for example, bin, lip.

- Explain how the long vowel sound is written in words like lie, pipe, high and try, that is, *ie*, *i-e*, *igh* and *y*.

- Write the following words on the board, showing the different representations of the long /igh/ sound: lie, fly, bite, night, time, cry, die, flight. Ask the children to read the words and put them into four lists. What do they notice about the words in the four lists?

  Notes: *y is usually found at the end of words. There are a few exceptions, for example, tie, die, lie, pie. These words should be directly taught and learned.*

  igh is usually found in the middle of words, followed by the letter 't', with some exceptions. (Bite, kite and white are the exceptions the children at this stage are most likely to use.)

  y and igh can both be taught through onset and rime.

- *i-e* is the more common representation of the long *i* in the middle of words (remembering that *igh* is used when followed by 't'). Elicit from the children words with the *i-e* representation and write them on the board.

- Give practice in writing words with the long /igh/ sound. Using individual whiteboards and pens, ask the children to write words in groups that you dictate. This will reinforce letter sequence and motor memory.

- Encourage the children to apply their knowledge about the different representations of the long /igh/ sound when spelling.

Practise–Explore–Investigate

- Distribute *i-e*, *igh*, *ie* and *y* phoneme cards. Say examples of words with the long /igh/ sound represented by *i-e*, *igh*, *ie* and *y*. Ask the children to hold up the phoneme card that represents the long /igh/ sound in the word they hear.

- Challenge the children to make lists of words which have the different representations of the long /igh/ sound, *i-e*, *igh*, *ie*, *y*. Encourage the use of onset and rime as a strategy for spelling.

- Ask the children to exchange their list with a partner and discuss any misspelled words to arrive at the correct spelling. Encourage the children to refer back to the rule.

Introductory Pupil Book

pages 14–15

Introductory Practice Book

page 7

Resource Sheet 6

A

B

Enrichment

- Investigate other representations of the long /igh/ sound, such as I, eye, bye, buy. Write a list of approximately 16 words, including I, eye, bye and buy. Ask the children to identify any words that have different representations of the long vowel sound *i*. Ask the children what they notice about each pair of words, I and eye, bye and buy – they sound the same but are spelled differently.

- Ask the children to use the words orally to show that they understand the different meanings of the words in each pair.

  Note: *words that sound the same but have different spellings are called homophones.*

- Also investigate sigh, high and thigh, where *igh* is at the end of the word. Write the words high, sigh and thigh on the board. Ask the children to think of their previous learning, *igh* often appears in the middle of words followed by the letter *t*. This does not apply to the above words.

Apply–Assess–Reflect AfL

- Give the children the opportunity to reflect on their learning.
- Elicit the key points:
    - the differences between the short and long vowels *i*, *igh* (encourage the children to give examples)
    - the different ways to write the long vowel /igh/ in words (encourage the children to give examples).
- Ask the children to write two examples of words with each letter pattern *ie*, *igh*, *i-e*, *y* and to underline the vowel phoneme (long vowel sound).

Dictation

1. I saw the moon in the sky last night.
2. The bright light made the baby cry.
3. He has a blue and white tie.
4. I will clean and shine my bike next week.
5. I had a meat pie for tea.

Word Book

- Encourage the children to add new or challenging words to *My Third Word Book*.

Answers

Introductory Pupil Book

pages 14–15

Getting started

Write a word to name each picture. Circle the letters that make the long *i* sound.

1. r(igh)t
2. fl(y)
3. f(igh)t
4. sl(i)d(e)
5. t(ie)
6. k(i)t(e)
7. t(igh)t
8. p(ie)
9. n(i)n(e)

More to think about

Use the clues to work out the words. Circle the letters that make the long *i* sound.

1. a woman on her wedding day

    br(i)d(e)

2. nervous about meeting people

    sh(y)

3. the brightness from the sun, moon, fires or lamps

    l(igh)t

4. your backbone

    sp(i)n(e)

5. a long narrow piece of cloth, worn with a shirt

    t(ie)

6. a hut with a yard, where pigs are kept

    st(y)

Now try these

1. Rhyming helps with spelling. Change the first sound to make two more rhyming words each time.

    Possible answers:
    a) -ight   night → *light* → *sight*
    b) -y   sky → *cry* → *try*
    c) -ide   hide → *side* → *tide*

2. Choose one word from each group. Write three sentences, each using a different word. *(Children's own answers.)*

Introductory Practice Book

page 7

A 1. nine   2. *cry*
   3. *tie*   4. *fight*

B 1. fly, *my, cry*
   2. *line, dine, mine, pine, fine*
   3. *lie, die, pie*
   4. *flight, light, might, fight*

Resource Sheet 6

A 1. l(igh)t   2. cr(y)   3. fl(y)
   4. l(i)n(e)   5. p(ie)   6. t(ie)

B 1. *flight*   2. *dry*   3. *die*
   4. *time*

Progress Unit 1

Answers

A Write the words. They all contain the long vowel sound *a*.

1. *snail*
2. *snake*
3. *plate*
4. *tray*
5. *chain*
6. *paint*

B Write the words. They all contain the long vowel sound *o*.

1. *bow*
2. *goat*
3. *snow*
4. *rope*
5. *smoke*
6. *boat*

C Write the words. They all contain the long vowel sound *e*.

1. *sweet*
2. *lead*
3. *teeth*
4. *peach*
5. *leek*
6. *seal*

D Write the words. They all contain the long vowel sound *i* or *u*.

1. *pie*
2. *pipe*
3. *stool*
4. *tube*
5. *fly*
6. *screw*

Planning

- **Unit focus**
  To identify the common spelling pattern for the short vowel phoneme oo and to spell words with this spelling pattern

- **Learning objective**
  Spell new words using phonics as the prime approach

- **Support for Spelling**
  Y2 Term 1 (i): To secure the reading and spelling of words containing different spellings for phonemes

  CPL: Big Book 2C Unit 10 Morris Plays Hide and Seek
  CPL: Big Book 2C Unit 10 Mountain Mona

Introduction

Overview

This unit builds upon and consolidates a programme of discrete phonic teaching.

By the end of the unit, the children should be secure in their knowledge and understanding of the alternative spellings for the short vowel sound /oo/.

Rule

The letters *oo* and *u* often make the same sound (phoneme): crook, bully.

Note: this can vary according to dialect/accent.

Revisit–Explain–Use

- Select a short paragraph such as the one below. The paragraph should include examples of words where the letter *u* represents the short vowel sound /u/ and words where the letter *u* represents the long vowel sound /oo/. Enlarge, display and read to the children.

  'I had to run to the bus stop. I put my hand out to stop the bus but the bus was full and did not stop.'

- Reread the paragraph, asking the children to identify words that have the same written vowel making two different sounds.

  Examples
  run   put
  bus   full
  but

- Elicit from the children that the same letter 'u' can represent different sounds.

Teach–Model–Define

- Write the following words on the board: good, foot, crook, pull, bull, full, push.

- Investigate with the children what these words have in common. The words have the same sound represented by different letters *oo* and *u*.

  Notes: *care should be taken here as dialect can affect the pronunciation of words with* oo *– it can be short as in good or long as in cool. The words pull, bull, full, push and put should be memorised for their spelling pattern.*

- Ensure that the children know the correct usage of pull and full and compare with pool and fool.

- Give children practice in writing words with the *oo* letter pattern.

  Examples
stood	book
good	cook
wood	look
hook	wool
took	foot
brook	

- Give practice in writing words where oo represents the long /(y)oo/ sound, and compare with the words studied in the previous activity. Using individual whiteboards and pens, ask the children to write words in groups that you dictate. This will reinforce letter sequence and motor memory.

  Examples
food	room
mood	broom
fool	soon
tool	moon
cool	spoon
pool	boot
stool	shoot
school	root

Practise–Explore–Investigate

- Challenge the children to make lists of words which contain either *oo* or *u*, the different representations of the short *oo* sound.

- Ask the children to exchange their list with a partner and discuss any misspelled words to arrive at the correct spelling. Encourage children to refer back to the rule.

Introductory Pupil Book

pages 18–19

Resource Sheet 7

Enrichment

- Investigate with the children the words could, would and should where the short *oo* sound is represented by *ou*. Give the children the words could, would and should in a list and ask them to read the words. Ask what they notice about how the short *oo* sound is written in the words – by the letters *ou*.

- Ask the children to write the words could, would and should, focusing on onset and rime.

- Ask the children to orally give a sentence for each word.

Apply–Assess–Reflect AfL

- Give the children the opportunity to reflect on their learning.

- Elicit the key point:
  - there are different ways to write the short /oo/ vowel in words *oo/u* (encourage the children to give examples).

- Ask the children to write two examples of words with *u*, (for example, put) and words with *oo* (for example, took).

Dictation

1. She put the toast on the plate.
2. He took the wood to make a gate.
3. The bull stood in the shed.
4. I had to push the bike out of the woods.
5. I will read the book next week.

Word Book

- Encourage the children to add new or challenging words to *My Third Word Book*.

Answers

Introductory Pupil Book

pages 18–19

Getting started

Write a word to name each picture.

1. wood   2. *pull*   3. *look*

4. *wool*   5. *bull*   6. *book*

7. *hook*   8. *full*   9. *foot*

More to think about

Choose the correct word to complete each sentence.

1. Asam had to pull the sledge up the hill.

2. Tom shouted, "April *fool*!" when he played the trick.

3. I swam to the deep end of the *pool*.

4. This box is *full* of sweets!

Now try these

1. Add the letters to make words.
   a) look, *took, brook, shook*
   b) *good, hood, stood, wood*

2. Choose one -*ook* word and one -*ood* word. Write a sentence using each one.
   (Children's own answers.)

Resource Sheet 7

contains *oo*	contains *u*
wool	*pull*
book	*put*
foot	*push*
good	*full*
stood	*bull*

Words with *ar*

Planning

- **Unit focus**

  To identify the common spelling pattern for the phoneme *ar* and to spell words with this spelling pattern

- **Learning objective**

  Spell new words using phonics as the prime approach

- **Support for Spelling**

  Y4 Term 2 (i) To investigate and learn to spell words with common letter strings

  CPL: Big Book 2B Unit 6 Jelly on a Plate

Introduction

Overview

This unit builds upon and consolidates a programme of discrete phonic teaching.

By the end of the unit, the children should be secure in their knowledge and understanding of the letter string *ar*.

Developing an eye for common letter strings, and their most likely positions in words, is a useful aid for correct spelling.

Rule

The sound made by the letter string *ar* sounds like the alphabet name R: car.

Revisit–Explain–Use

Note: A letter string is a sequence of letters that occurs frequently. Children will already be familiar with some letter strings and where they are most likely to appear in words (for example, ay, ow, ai, oa).

- Discuss with the children letters that often appear together in words, for example, *sh*, *ch*, *th*, *oo*, *igh*.

Teach–Model–Define

 Word list 8

- Write the letter *r* on the board. Establish what the name of the letter is. Write the word car on the board and elicit which sounds can be easily heard in the word car, these are, *c* and *r*.

- Remind the children that all words must have a vowel or the letter *y*. Establish that the vowel in car is *a* and that *ar* represents the sound after the letter *c* in car.

  Note: *Missing out the vowel or writing the wrong vowel is a common error in words where a vowel is followed by the letter* r. *Again, dialect can influence pronunciation considerably.*

- Give children practice in writing words with the *ar* letter pattern. Encourage the use of onset and rime.

  Examples

car	art	arm	card	ark
bar	cart	farm	hard	bark
jar	tart	harm	lard	dark
far	part	charm	yard	hark
tar	start			lark
star	chart			mark
	smart			park
				spark
				shark

Practise–Explore–Investigate

- Play 'Find a rime'. Distribute a word card (using words from the Examples list in 'Teach–Model–Define') to each child. Ask the children to find a word that rimes with their word. Each pair should then find another pair who have words that rime with their words. Repeat until groups are complete.

- When sorted into groups, ask each child in turn to read their word aloud. Encourage speed and accuracy.

- Ask the children to make lists of rhyming words for the following rimes: -ar, -art, -arm, -ark, -ard.

- Ask the children to exchange their list with a partner and discuss any misspelled words to arrive at the correct spelling.

Introductory Pupil Book

pages 20–21

Introductory Practice Book

page 8

Enrichment

- Investigate with the children words where other vowels (*e, i, o* and *u*) join with the letter *r*, such as herd, girl, born, curl. Tell the children that the other vowels can come before the letter *r* in words, for example,

  er as in her
  ir as in bird
  or as in born
  ur as in curl.

- Distribute -er, -ir, -or and -ur cards. Say words such as herd, girl, bird, curl, her, burn, torn and horn. Ask the children to hold up the card that represents the sound that they can hear in the middle of each word.

Apply–Assess–Reflect AfL

- Give the children the opportunity to reflect on their learning.
- Elicit the key points:
  - a letter string is a sequence of letters in a word (encourage the children to give examples)
  - *ar* is a letter string. Encourage the children to give examples of words with the letter string *ar*.
- Ask the children to write two examples of words with the letter string *ar*.

Dictation

1. We went in the car to the park.
2. We will play a game of cards.
3. The cart is in the farmyard.
4. It is hard to see in the dark.
5. I made a jam tart.

Word Book

Encourage the children to add new or challenging words to *My Third Word Book*.

Answers

Introductory Pupil Book

pages 20–21

Getting started

Write a word to name each picture.

1. park
2. *car*
3. *star*
4. *jar*
5. *go-kart*
6. *tart*
7. *card*
8. *dart*
9. *shark*

More to think about

Add letters to make words.

1. far, *car, jar, bar*
2. *smart, chart, cart, part*
3. *dark, lark, mark, spark*
4. *lard, hard, yard, card*

Now try these

Use the clues to work out the words. Circle the letters that make the *ar* sound in each word.

1. a round pastry case with a fruit filling

   t(ar)t
2. the third month of the year

   M(ar)ch
3. a thick covering for a floor, often made of wool

   c(ar)pet
4. a place where people buy and sell things

   m(ar)ket
5. land next to a house where people can grow things

   g(ar)den
6. the gathering of crops when they are ripe

   h(ar)vest

Introductory Practice Book

page 8

A *Possible answers:*

1. bar, car, *far, jar, tar, star*
2. part, *cart, dart, tart, chart, start, smart*
3. *park, bark, dark, lark, mark, hark, shark*

B 1. *arm*

2. *armour*

Oi and oy

Planning

- **Unit focus**

  To identify the common spelling patterns for the vowel phoneme *oi* (*oi/oy*) and to spell words with these spelling patterns

- **Learning objectives**

  Spell new words using phonics as the prime approach

  Recognise and use alternative ways of spelling the phonemes already taught

- **Support for Spelling**

  Y4 Term 2 (i): To investigate and learn to spell words with common letter strings

  CPL: Big Book 2A Unit 3 Funky Feet

Introduction

Overview

This unit builds upon and consolidates a programme of discrete phonic teaching.

By the end of the unit, the children should be secure in their knowledge and understanding of the alternative spellings for the vowel phoneme represented by *oi/oy*.

Rule

The letters *oi* and *oy* often make the same sound.

The letters *oi* are often found in the middle of words: coin.

The letters *oy* are often found at the end of words: boy.

Revisit–Explain–Use

- Orally revise the different written representations of the long vowel sounds.

/ai/	*ai, ay, a-e*
/oa/	*oa, ow, o-e*
/ee/	*ee, ea*
/(y)oo/	*oo, ew, ue ,u-e*
/igh/	*igh, ie, i-e, y*

  Distribute phoneme 'show me' cards *ai*, *ay*, and *a-e*. Say words, for example, train, cake, play, chain, tray, say, tame. Ask the children to hold up the correct card that represents the /ai/ sound, that is, *ai*, *ay*, or *a-e*.

- Repeat the activity for the long vowel sounds /oa/, /ee/, /oo/, /igh/.

Teach–Model–Define

- Select sentences such as the examples below. The sentences should include examples of words where the sound /oi/ is represented by the letters *oi* and *oy*. Enlarge, display and read to the children.

  Examples
  'Roy has a pound coin.'
  'He did not spoil the toy car.'

- Reread the sentences asking the children to identify words that have the same sound written in the two different ways.

  Examples
  Roy   coin
  toy   spoil

- Practice auditory discrimination. Invite the children to listen for the *oi* sound in words. Is it heard in the middle or the end of the word? Write the words on the board.

  Examples
  coin
  boy
  join
  coil
  toy
  Roy
  boil

- Investigate with the children which letter combinations represent the *oi* sound.

  Note: oi *is used in the middle of words and* oy *at the end of words (or at the end of a syllable in multi-syllable words) – see 'Enrichment'.*

- Distribute [oy] and [oi] 'show me' cards and invite children to hold up the card that represents the *oi* sound in words that you say aloud. Alternatively whiteboards or blank pieces of paper can be used – and the children can write *oy* or *oi*.

  Examples
hoist	toy
Troy	annoy
join	coin
coy	enjoy
boy	destroy
point	spoil
joint	moist

- Give the children practice in writing dictated *oi/oy* words.

Practise–Explore–Investigate

- Challenge the children to make lists of words that have the letters *oi* or *oy* in them.

- Ask the children to exchange lists with a partner and discuss any misspelled words to arrive at the correct spelling. Encourage children to refer back to the rule.

Introductory Pupil Book

pages 22–23

Introductory Practice Book

page 9

Enrichment

- Investigate with children words like royal, loyal, oyster, voyage. Although *oy* does not appear at the end of the words it is at the end of the first syllable. Say the words royal, loyal, oyster, voyage in 'slow speak' emphasising the two syllables.

- Ask the children what they notice about the words – they all have two syllables.

- Discuss with the children the spelling of the first syllable of each word. Is it more likely to be *oi* or *oy*? Why?

  Note: *words in the English language don't often have three vowels together.*

Apply–Assess–Reflect AfL

- Give the children the opportunity to reflect on their learning.
- Elicit the key points:
  - the same sound can be written in different ways
  - *oi* and *oy* can represent the same sound (encourage the children to give examples).
- Ask the children to write two examples of words with each sound *oi* and *oy*. Ask them to underline the vowel phoneme.

Dictation

1. The boy lost a coin in the soil.
2. He can join the club when he is nine.
3. She made a star with five points.
4. We will join the rope to the bar on the cart.
5. Coil the rope before you put it away.

Word Book

Encourage the children to add new or challenging words to *My Third Word Book*.

Answers

Introductory Pupil Book

pages 22–23

Getting started

1. Write the words.
   a) t + o = toy
   b) j + oin = *join*
   c) b + oy = *boy*
   d) R + oy = *Roy*
   e) b + oil = *boil*
   f) s = oil = *soil*
   g) p + oint = *point*
   h) j + oy = *joy*
   i) c + oil = *coil*

2. Say the words from Question 1. Where do you hear the *oi/oy* sound – in the middle or at the end? Write the words in the table.

Middle	End
join	toy
boil	boy
soil	Roy
point	joy
coil	

3. Look at the words in each column. What do you notice?
   Join, boil, soil, point and coil all have oi *in the middle. Toy, boy, Roy and joy all have* oy *at the end and they rime.*

More to think about

Write these signs correctly.

1. *Join* the club here
2. Fine top *soil*
3. *Boys*
4. *Boil* in a bag meal: buy one get one free!
5. *Coins* only
6. *Toys* for sale

Now try these

Find ten *oi* and *oy* words in the wordsearch. Write each word in the correct column. Two have been done to help you.

oi	oy
joint	coy
coin	toy
point	joy
spoil	boy(s)
join	
coil	

Introductory Practice Book

page 9

A 1. *Possible answers:*
   boy
   toy
   joy

   2. *Possible answers:*
   boil   *spoil*
   toil   *foil*
   coil   *soil*

B 1. *enjoy*   2. *annoy*
   3. *royal*   4. *destroy*

60

Ou and ow

Planning

- **Unit focus**

  To identify the common spelling patterns for the vowel phoneme *ou* and *ow* and to spell words with these spelling patterns

- **Learning objective**

  Spell new words using phonics as the prime approach

- **Support for Spelling**

  Y2 Term 1 (i): To secure the reading and spelling of words containing different spellings for phonemes

  Y4 Term 2 (i): To investigate and learn to spell words with common letter strings

  > **CPL: Big Book 2C** Unit 10 Morris Plays Hide and Seek
  > **CPL: Big Book 2C** Unit 10 Mountain Mona

Introduction

Overview

This unit builds upon and consolidates a programme of discrete phonic teaching.

By the end of the unit, the children should be secure in their knowledge and understanding of the alternative spellings for the vowel phoneme represented by *ou/ow*.

Developing an eye for common letter strings, and their most likely positions in words, is a useful aid for correct spelling.

Rule

The letters *ou* and *ow* can make the same sound: house, cow.

Revisit–Explain–Use

- Orally revise the different written representations for the *oi* sound, that is, *oi* and *oy* (see Unit 9).

Teach–Model–Define

- Select a sentence such as the example below. The sentences should include examples of words where the sound /ou/ is represented by the letters *ou* and the letters *ow*.

- Enlarge, display and read it to the children.

  'A brown owl looked down at a mouse coming out from his house.'

Word list 10

- Reread the sentence asking the children to identify words that have the same sound written in two different ways.

brown	mouse
owl	out
down	house

- Write the following words on the board: cow, now, how, town, crown, cloud, shout, round.

  Explain that *ow* and *ou* are both used in the middle of words, but *ou* is never used at the end of words – always use *ow* (except for older words like thou).

- Ask the children to help you sort the *ou* and *ow* words and look at the letter patterns that follow *ow* and *ou*. Ask the children to help you add other words to each list.

  Examples

cow	town	owl	towel
now	down	howl	vowel
how	gown	fowl	tower
row	frown	growl	power
bow	drown		flower
	brown	crowd	shower

loud	mouth	found	grout
cloud	south	hound	snout
proud		mound	stout
		round	trout
count	house	sound	spout
mount	mouse	wound	scout
		pound	shout

  Note: *It is usually safe to use* ou *before* nd, nt, t, d *(note crowd),* se *and* th.

- Give practice in writing these letter strings until they become automatic: *-own, -ower, -ound, -out, -oud, -ouse, -ount, -outh.* Using individual whiteboards and pens, ask the children to write words in groups that you dictate. This will reinforce letter sequence and motor memory.

- Investigate homophones like flower/flour and fowl/foul. Display pictures of a flower and flour. Ask the children to write the words for each picture.

  Check suggestions and establish the correct spellings.

- Play 'What are the words'? Give the children clues such as the following and ask them to write the words;
  – in sport, an action that breaks the rules
  – a bird, such as a chicken or a duck, that is kept or hunted for its meat or eggs.

- Encourage the children to use a dictionary to check spelling and meaning.

- Investigate the different pronunciations of *ow* in words like bow, sow, row. Display sentences showing the different meanings of bow, sow and row. Highlight bow, sow and row in the sentences. Ask the children to read sentences and elicit how they know which pronunciation of the highlighted words is correct.

  Note: *Ensure that children know that the surrounding text will determine the pronunciation of the word.*

Practise–Explore–Investigate

- Ask the children to generate lists of rhyming words with the following letter strings: *-oud, -ound, -out, -ow, -own, -owl, -ower.*

  Note: *Encourage the use of onset and rime as spelling strategies.*

- Ask the children to exchange their list with a partner and discuss any misspelled words to arrive at the correct spelling. Encourage children to refer back to the rule.

Introductory Pupil Book

pages 24–25

Introductory Practice Book

page 10

Resource Sheet 10

Enrichment

- Investigate with the children words that have the letters *ou* but make a different sound, such as shoulder, boulder, coupon, mouldy, soul, could, would, should. Ask the children to work in pairs. Give each pair of children cards with the above words written on them. Ask the children to read the words aloud and to sort them into groups, according to how the *ou* sound in each word is pronounced. Encourage the children to read the groups of words aloud.

- Investigate the homonym wound. Look at the word 'wound' and elicit the two ways that it can be pronounced. Ask the children to work in pairs to orally make up two sentences to show the different meanings of 'wound'.

- Tell the children that words that have the same spellings but different meanings are called homonyms.

Apply–Assess–Reflect AfL

- Give the children the opportunity to reflect on their learning.
- Elicit the key points:
  - the same sound can be written in different ways
  - *ou* and *ow* can represent the same sound (encourage the children to give examples).
- Ask the children to write two examples of words for each letter pattern *ou*, *ow* and to underline the vowel phoneme.

Dictation

1. A brown owl flew out of the tree.
2. I found a pound coin on the ground.
3. There are a few clouds in the blue sky.
4. The shower of rain was good for the flowers.
5. He felt proud as he took a bow.

Word Book WB

Encourage the children to add new or challenging words to *My Third Word Book*.

Answers

Introductory Pupil Book

pages 24–25

Getting started

1. Write a word to name each picture.
   a) clown b) *crown* c) *owl*
   d) *crowd* e) *frown* f) *bow*
2. Complete these sentences with *ow* words.
   a) He drove too fast *down* the hill.
   b) In autumn, some leaves turn *brown*.

More to think about

Add letters to make new words.

Possible answers:

1. hound, *ground, found, pound, round, sound*
2. brown, *clown, crown, down, drown, town*

Now try these

1. Write a word to name each picture.
   a) cloud b) *house* c) *spout*
2. Complete these sentences with *ou* words.
   a) Tom found a *pound* coin.
   b) A circle is a *round* shape.
   c) Mum will *count* the money after the sale.
   d) She fell on the *ground* and hurt her leg.
   e) Mark had to *shout* for help.
   f) The cat chased the *mouse*.
   g) The brass band played *loud* music.
   h) The opposite of north is *south*.

Introductory Practice Book

page 10

Possible answers:

1. **c**ow, *how, row, now, bow, sow*
2. **d**own, *clown, frown, crown, drown, town, gown, brown*
3. **t**ower, *shower, power, flower, glower*
4. **p**ound, *hound, found, sound, round, mound, bound, ground*
5. **st**out, *clout, bout, flout, lout, shout, trout, grout*

Resource Sheet 10

1. owls
2. *Trout*
3. *Scout*
4. *Clouds*
5. *vowels*
6. *Ground*
7. *Crown*
8. *Flowers*

Adding -*s*

Planning

- **Unit focus**

  To use the word ending -*s* (plural) to support reading and spelling

- **Learning objectives**

  Spell new words using phonics as the prime approach

  Use knowledge of common inflections in spelling, such as plurals

- **Support for Spelling**

  Y2 Term 2 (ii): To learn how to add common inflections (suffixes) to words e.g. plurals

- **Grammar, Punctuation and Spelling Test references**

  sg/ga7.8, sg/ga7.9

  > **CPL: Big Book 2C** Unit 8 Index of Eggs and Chicks
  > **CPL: Big Book 2C** Unit 8 Using This Dictionary
  > **CPL: Big Book 2C** Unit 9 Two Tongue-twisters
  >
  > **CPF: Grammar and Punctuation Introductory Pupil Book:** Unit 12 Singular and plural

Introduction

Overview

This unit builds upon and consolidates a programme of discrete phonic teaching.

By the end of the unit, the children should be secure in their knowledge and understanding of how to make words plural by adding *s*.

An inflection is a particular kind of suffix. We use inflectional suffixes to turn nouns into plurals, for example, boat → boats

Rule

Most words add -*s* to make plurals: cat → cats.

Revisit–Explain–Use

Notes: Before teaching the children to spell plural words, it is important that they understand the concepts of singular and plural.

See Collins Primary Focus: Grammar and Punctuation Introductory Pupil Book Unit 12 for an introduction to this concept.

- Explain that singular means one and plural means more than one.

- Invite the children to give the plural form of singular words that they can see around them.

  Examples

book(s)	pen(s)	table(s)
cup(s)	boy(s)	cake(s)

Teach–Model–Define

- Write a selection of singular and plural words on the board, where the plural is made by adding -s.

  Examples
  book → books
  shop → shops
  fan → fans
  wheel → wheels
  cake → cakes
  train → trains

- Investigate the difference between each pair of words. Establish that -s has been added to make singular words plural. Ensure that children know and use the terms 'singular' and 'plural'.

- Play 'Singular/plural chain'. Ask the children to sit in circles (with eight to ten children in each circle). The first child says a singular word, such as book. The second child says the plural of that word (books). The third child gives a new plural word, such as gates. The fourth child has to give the singular form (gate). The fifth child gives a new singular word. The children should try to complete the circle without breaking the chain.

- Give practice in writing the singular and plural form of words where -s is added to make the plural. Using individual whiteboards and pens, ask the children to write words that you dictate.

Practise–Explore–Investigate

- Give the children lists of nouns. Ask the children to write the plural form by adding s.

  Examples

  | tray | game | chair | boat | clown |
  | light | boy | sweet | cloud | seat |

- Ask the children to exchange their list with a partner and discuss any misspelled words to arrive at the correct spelling. Encourage children to refer back to the rule. Ask the children to point out the vowel phonemes in each word.

Introductory Pupil Book

pages 26–27

Resource Sheet 11

Enrichment

- Investigate with the children words that form the plural by adding -es. Ask the children to find examples of plural words ending in -es in their reading books. In groups, the children should collect their words and then write the singular form of each word. Ask what they notice (that words ending in x, s, sh and ch take -es in the plural).

  fox + es = foxes
  bus + es = buses
  crash + es = crashes
  church + es = churches

  Note: when -es is added to singular words that end in -s, -x and -sh to make the plural form, the plural form has an extra syllable, for example, foxes, brushes, buses.

- Ask the children to use their plural words to write a short poem, short story or sentence, depending on ability.

Apply–Assess–Reflect AfL

- Give the children the opportunity to reflect on their learning.
- Elicit the key point:
  - for most nouns you add an *s* to form the plural.
- Ask the children to write two examples of words where *s* is added to make the word plural.

Dictation

1. She made nine jars of jam and five cakes.
2. We went out in boats to see the seals.
3. The boys can play on the swings in the park.
4. The nests are made of twigs and moss.
5. I need three plates and spoons.

Word Book

Encourage the children to add new or challenging words to *My Third Word Book*.

Answers

Introductory Pupil Book

pages 26–27

Getting started

Add -*s* to make each word plural.

1. hat + s = hats
2. mop + s = *mops*
3. dog + s = *dogs*
4. bun + s = *buns*
5. hut + s = *huts*
6. pin + s = *pins*
7. van + s = *vans*
8. doll + s = *dolls*
9. lid + s = *lids*
10. pen + s = *pens*
11. bed + s = *beds*
12. net + s = *nets*
13. bell + s = *bells*
14. fan + s = *fans*
15. pram + s = *prams*
16. frog + s = *frogs*
17. ring + s = *rings*
18. clock + s = *clocks*
19. shop + s = *shops*
20. chair + s = *chairs*

More to think about

Write a plural word to name each picture.

1. tents
2. *hands*
3. *drums*
4. *cuffs*
5. *nests*
6. *flags*
7. *plums*
8. *crabs*
9. *rafts*

Now try these

Copy these sentences. Make the underlined words plural.

1. Jan jumped in the puddles.
2. Mandy shut the *doors* to the *rooms*.
3. The *sweets* fell onto the *steps*.
4. I put the *books* on the *tables*.
5. The *boys* and *girls* played with the *toys*.

Resource Sheet 11

1. cat — cats
2. *wheel* — *wheels*
3. *snail* — *snails*
4. *seal* — *seals*
5. *vest* — *vests*
6. *hand* — *hands*
7. *boat* — *boats*
8. *tie* — *ties*

Unit 12

Adding -ed and -ing

Planning

- **Unit focus**

  To use the word endings -ed (past) and -ing (present) to support reading and spelling

- **Learning objectives**

  Spell new words using phonics as the prime approach

  Use knowledge of common inflections in spelling

- **Support for Spelling**

  Y2 Term 1 (ii): To understand and begin to learn the conventions for adding the suffix -ed for past tense and -ing for present tense

- **Grammar, Punctuation and Spelling Test references**

  sg/ga4.1, sg/ga7.8

  CPL: Big Book 2B Unit 7 The Last Noo-Noo
  CPL: Big Book 2B Unit 7 The Worst Witch

  CPF: Grammar and Punctuation Introductory Pupil Book Unit 5 Verbs, Unit 11 Verbs (past tense)

Introduction

Overview

This unit builds upon and consolidates a programme of discrete phonic teaching. By the end of the unit, the children should be secure in their knowledge and understanding of the conventions for adding the suffix -ed for past tense and -ing for present tense.

An inflection is a particular kind of suffix. We use inflection suffixes to alter the tense of verbs, for example:

look → looks → looking → looked.

Before teaching the children to spell past tense verb forms, it is important that they understand about the class of words described as verbs and the meaning of past and present in relation to tense.

Rule

For most words just add -ed or -ing:

bark → barked → barking.

Revisit–Explain–Use

- Establish that the children understand what a verb is.

  Note: Collins Primary Focus: Grammar and Punctuation Introductory Pupil Book *Units 5 and 11 provide an introduction to verbs and the past tense.*

- Play oral games that require the children to change the tense from present to past and the reverse.

  Examples

  Today I am painting. Yesterday I painted
  Yesterday I skated, today I am _____
  Today it is snowing. Yesterday it _____

  What are you doing today?
  A child replies: I am washing the car.
                  I am reading a book.
  What did you do yesterday?
  A child replies: I walked to the shops.
                  I washed my hair.

Teach–Model–Define

- Write pairs of present and past tense verbs on the board.

  Examples
  jump → jumped
  lock → locked
  push → pushed
  bark → barked
  pull → pulled

- Investigate the difference between each pair of words: *-ed* has been added to the root word to form the past tense of the verb.

  Notes: *It can be difficult for children to remember the* e *when adding* -ed *as it is not always heard in speech.*

  Another common mistake can be adding t *to make the past tense, for example, jumpt. A mnemonic that might help here is: 'Never d never t. Always add ed'.*

- Investigate with children words like landed and hunted where a second syllable can be clearly heard when *-ed* is added to land and hunt. Other words like this are lifted, mended, panted, shouted, painted, toasted.

- Use the same verbs and add *-ing* to the root word. Look carefully at each pair of words:
  – one ends in *-ing* and one ends in *-ed*
  – each word now has two syllables.

- Ask the children to identify syllables by clapping: jump/ing, bend/ing, shout/ing, paint/ing, clean/ing.

  Note: *It is important that children know that if they can spell, for example, jump, they can spell jumping by adding* -ing.

- Give practice in writing regular verbs with *-ed* and *-ing* endings. Using individual whiteboards and pens, ask the children to write words that you dictate. Monitor where any errors might occur, with the root word or with the ending.

Practise–Explore–Investigate

- Have two flash cards to hand, one with the word 'today' and the other with the word 'yesterday'. Tell the children that you will hold up one of the cards and say a word (verb). The children should add (*-ed*) or (*-ing*) to the verb to make a new word that fits with today/tomorrow.

- Give practice orally and then ask the children to write the answer (verbs), for example:

  'today'   rush → rushing
  'yesterday'   rush → rushed

  Examples

rush	faint	jump	mark
crack	roast	land	play
bang	shout	cool	drown
dust	point	need	join

Introductory Pupil Book

pages 28–29

Introductory Practice Book

page 11

Resource Sheet 12

Enrichment

- Investigate with the children words in which the last consonant is doubled before adding *-ed* or *-ing*. Write the following words on the board:

  rob → robbed → robbing
  pat → patted → patting
  hop → hopped → hopping
  hug → hugged → hugging.

  Ask the children to read the words and say what they notice about them.

  Is there a pattern? Help the children to deduce what the rule might be when adding *-ed* or *-ing* to words like hop.

- Ask the children to suggest any other words that might fit the pattern, for example, wag, rip, mop, jog, sob, drop, chop, skip. Ask the children to choose three of the suggested words and write them in the pattern of:

  rob → robbed → robbing.

Apply–Assess–Reflect AfL

- Give the children the opportunity to reflect on their learning.
- Elicit the key points:
  - -ed and -ing are suffixes
  - suffixes are added to the end of words (encourage the children to give examples)
  - adding -ed to a verb changes the tense of the verb to the past.
- Ask the children to write two examples of words with each suffix -ed, -ing.

Dictation

1. He lifted the mouse in his hands.
2. She pushed the cart down the hill.
3. The plane landed on the ground.
4. The crowd are shouting for the game to start.
5. The girls are playing in the farmyard.

Word Book WB

Encourage the children to add new or challenging words to *My Third Word Book*.

Answers

Introductory Pupil Book

pages 28–29

Getting started

1. Add -ed to each word to make a new word.
   a) rush → rushed
   b) land → *landed*
   c) open → *opened*
   d) play → *played*
   e) jump → *jumped*
   f) push → *pushed*
   g) pull → *pulled*
   h) want → *wanted*
   i) lick → *licked*
   j) moan → *moaned*
   k) sail → *sailed*
   l) crash → *crashed*

2. Add -ing to each word to make a new word.
   a) eat → *eating*
   b) lift → *lifting*
   c) send → *sending*
   d) lock → *locking*
   e) melt → *melting*
   f) sing → *singing*
   g) kick → *kicking*
   h) sell → *selling*
   i) jump → *jumping*
   j) bring → *bringing*
   k) stand → *standing*
   l) crack → *cracking*

More to think about

Copy and complete the table.

Root word	Add -ed	Add -ing
lick	*licked*	*licking*
look	*looked*	*looking*
sail	*sailed*	*sailing*
float	*floated*	*floating*
glow	*glowed*	*glowing*
bang	*banged*	*banging*
rest	*rested*	*resting*
shift	*shifted*	*shifting*
park	*parked*	*parking*

Now try these

Choose the correct word to complete the sentences.

1. Nick is pulling the rope.
2. He *locked* the door of the shed.
3. Jaz *helped* to pack the case.
4. Wes *kicked* the ball in the net.
5. Kerry is *playing* with a friend.

Introductory Practice Book

page 11

1. pack, packed, packing
2. *link, linked, linking*
3. *brush, brushed, brushing*
4. *push, pushed, pushing*
5. *pull, pulled, pulling*
6. *want, wanted, wanting*
7. *ask, asked, asking*
8. *crack, cracked, cracking*

Resource Sheet 12

1. He is kicking.
2. She *planted* the bulbs.
3. He *shouted* to me.
4. They are *reading*.
5. She is *jumping*.
6. They *cooked* a meal.
7. She *lifted* the box.
8. She is *painting*.

Progress Unit 2

Answers

A Write a word to name each picture.

1. *cook*
2. *bull*
3. *shark*
4. *star*
5. *wool*
6. *dart*

B Write a word to name each picture.

1. *coin*
2. *cloud*
3. *boy*
4. *clown*
5. *owl*
6. *mouse*

C Write the singular and plural forms of each word.

1. one *drum*, two *drums*
2. one *bed*, two *beds*
3. one *car*, two *cars*
4. one *spoon*, two *spoons*
5. one *frog*, two *frogs*
6. one *wheel*, two *wheels*

D Copy and complete the table.

Root word	Add *-ed*	Add *-ing*
camp	*camped*	*camping*
land	*landed*	*landing*
melt	*melted*	*melting*
crack	*cracked*	*cracking*
brush	*brushed*	*brushing*
bark	*barked*	*barking*
play	*played*	*playing*
snow	*snowed*	*snowing*

Unit 13

Or, er, ir, ur, air and ear

Planning

- **Unit focus**

  To identify the common spelling patterns for the vowel phonemes *or*, *er*, and *air* and to spell words with these spelling patterns

- **Learning objective**

  Spell new words using phonics as the prime approach

- **Support for Spelling**

  Y4 Term 2 (ii): To investigate and learn to spell words with common letter strings

  CPL: Big Book 2A Unit 1 Class Six and the Very Big Rabbit

  CPL: Big Book 2B Unit 5 Snake Charm

Introduction

Overview

This unit builds upon and consolidates a programme of discrete phonic teaching.

By the end of the unit, the children should be secure in their knowledge and understanding of the letter strings *or*, *er*, *ir*, *ur*, *air* and *ear*.

Developing an eye for common letter strings, and their most likely positions in words, is a useful aid for correct spelling.

Rule

A letter string is a group of letters in a word.

Common letter strings are *or*, *er*, *ir*, *ur*, *air* and *ear*.

Revisit–Explain–Use

- Revise the spelling pattern *-ar* (see Unit 8) and invite the children to generate words with this spelling pattern.

Teach–Model–Define

- Investigate other spelling patterns by asking the children to generate and sort words for each spelling pattern, such as:

e + r = er
i + r = ir
o + r = or
u + r = ur

Examples

-er	-ir	-or	-ur
her	fir	fork	curl
herd	stir	cork	burn
fern	girl	horn	turn
term	first	born	burst
	third	short	church
	bird	stork	

Note: *Remind the children that all words must have a vowel (or the letter y). Missing out the vowel or writing the wrong vowel is a common error in words where a vowel is followed by the letter r. Dialect can influence pronunciation considerably.*

- Distribute [or] [er] [ir] [ur] and [ar] 'show me' cards and invite children to hold up the card that represents the vowel + r sound in words that you say aloud.

Examples

park	curl
shirt	her
girl	fern
short	skirt
bird	horn
fur	sharp
charm	term
cord	lord

- Look at the spelling patterns *ai + r = air* and *ea + r = ear* (as in dear). Invite the children to generate and sort words for each spelling pattern.

Examples

fair	dear	stair	hear
hair	fear	chair	near
pair	clear		gear
			year

Practise–Explore–Investigate

- Ask the children to generate lists of rhyming words with the endings *-ar, -er, -ir, -or, -ur, -ear, -air*.

- Ask them to exchange their list with a partner and discuss any misspelled words to arrive at the correct spelling.

Introductory Pupil Book

pages 32–33

Introductory Practice Book

page 12

Resource Sheet 13

Enrichment

- Investigate with the children other representations of *air* and *ear*, such as *-are* making homophones of *air* words and *-ere* making homophones of *ear* words. Ask the children to write the words in sentences so that the context clarifies the meaning of each spelling.

hare/hair   here/hear
stare/stair
pare/pair
fare/fair

Apply–Assess–Reflect AfL

- Give the children the opportunity to reflect on their learning.
- Elicit the key points:
  - a letter string is a sequence of letters in a word
  - *or*, *er*, *ir*, *ur*, *air* and *ear* are letter strings.
- Ask the children to write two examples of words with each letter string *or*, *er*, *ir*, *ur*, *air* and *air*.

Dictation

1. The girl has a thorn in her foot.
2. The pipe burst near the house.
3. This is his first term at school.
4. A stork is a white and black bird with long red legs.
5. Her name was first on the list.

Word Book W B

Encourage the children to add new or challenging words to *My Third Word Book*.

Answers

Introductory Pupil Book

pages 32–33

Getting started

1. Use the consonants in the box to make words. You can use the letters more than once.
   a)–c) lord, *ford, cord, sword*
   d)–f) fort, *sort, snort, short*
   g)–i) cork, *fork, stork*

2. Use the consonants in the box to make four more words.
   a)   corn
   b)–e) *born, horn, torn, thorn*

3. Which letters were not needed?
   j, q and s

More to think about

Write a word to name each picture.

1. kerb   2. *skirt*   3. *bird*
4. *nurse*   5. *fern*   6. *church*

Now try these

1. Write only the *air* words from the box.
   chair, fair, hair, stair, pair

2. Write only the *ear* words from the box.
   fear, dear, hear, near, clear, spear, shear

Introductory Practice Book

page 12

1. *kerb*   2. *bird*   3. *burst*
4. *chair*   5. *spear*   6. *first*
7. *cherry*   8. *fork*   9. *third*

Resource Sheet 13

contains *-or*	**contains *-ir***
sort	thirst
cord	dirt
born	shirt

contains *-air*	**contains *-ear***
stair	clear
fair	near
chair	fear

Wh, ph and ch

Planning

- **Unit focus**

  To spell words with the digraphs *wh*, *ph* and *ch* (as in Christopher)

- **Learning objective**

  Spell new words using phonics as the prime approach

- **Support for Spelling**

  Y4 Term 2 (i): To investigate and learn to spell words with common letter strings

  > **CPL: Big Book 2B** Unit 5 Eggs and Chicks
  > **CPL: Big Book 2B** Unit 6 Hot Food

Introduction

Overview

This unit builds upon and consolidates a programme of discrete phonic teaching.

By the end of the unit, the children should be secure in their knowledge and understanding of the digraphs *wh*, *ph* and *ch*.

Rule

Two letters can represent one sound (phoneme):

w + *h* → *wh*: wheel

p + *h* → *f*: photograph.

Sometimes *c* + *h* can make the sound *k*: chorus.

Revisit–Explain–Use

- Revise with the children the concept of two letters representing one sound (phoneme). Invite the children to give examples, for example, *sh*, *ch*, *oo*, *ai*, *oa*.

Teach–Model–Define

- Write words with the phonemes *wh*, *ph* and *ch* on the board.

  Examples

wheel	dolphin	chemist
whale	photo	Christmas
whip	elephant	character
whisper	graph	
whistle	alphabet	

- Investigate with the children which pair of letters make one sound in each word. Underline the *wh*, *ph*, *ch* letters and establish the sound that each represents.

  Notes: *The letter* w *as in watch and the letters* wh *as in whale make very similar sounds and it can be difficult for the children to differentiate between them. Dialect will again influence this.*

  The ph *words and the words where* ch *represents* k *listed above, are those that the children at this stage are most likely to use. They should be taught directly.*

- Ask the children to tell you the sound that the letters *ch* normally make, that is, *ch* as in chair.

- Practice auditory discrimination. Give practice in matching the sound to its written representation. Distribute [wh] and [w] 'show me' cards or use whiteboards. Say words starting with *wh* or *w* and ask the children to show (or write) *wh* or *w*.

  Examples

was	whisk
watch	wool
whisper	window
why	white
well	whale
where	wet

Practise–Explore–Investigate

- Challenge the children to make a list of words starting with the letter *w* and a list of words starting with the letters *wh*.

- Ask them to exchange their list with a partner and discuss any misspelled words to arrive at the correct spelling. Encourage the children to refer back to the rule.

Introductory Pupil Book

pages 34–35

Introductory Practice Book

page 13

Enrichment

- Investigate with children another sound that the letters *ch* can represent, for example, *sh* as in chef, chiffon, chute, machine and parachute. Say the words chef, chiffon, chute. Ask the children which letters usually make up the /sh/ sound – *s* and *h*.

- Remind the children that sometimes a sound can be written in different ways, for example, /ai/ can be written as *ai*, *ay* or *a-e*.

- Write the words chef, chiffon and chute on the board. Ask the children which letters make up the /sh/ sound in chef, chiffon and chute.

- Tell the children that you are thinking of two words that have the letters 'ch' in the middle making the /sh/ sound. Give clues:

  A _____ is a large piece of thin cloth. It has strings fixed to it so that a person attached to it can float down to the ground from an aircraft.

  A _____ is a piece of equipment which does a particular kind of work. It is usually powered by an engine or by electricity.

  Write 'parachute' and 'machine' on the board.

- Ask the children to choose one of the five words (chef, chiffon, chute, machine and parachute). Ask them to write the word and illustrate it to display as a visual aid showing the sound /sh/ represented by *ch*.

Apply–Assess–Reflect AfL

- Give the children the opportunity to reflect on their learning.

- Elicit the key points:
  - two letters can represent one sound (encourage the children to give examples)
  - the same two letters *ch* can represent different sounds, for example, *ch* as in chair, *k* as in chemist.

- Ask the children to write three words, one word with the letters *wh*, one with the letters *ph* and one with the letters *ch*.

Dictation

1. Dolphins and whales live in the sea.
2. The Christmas tree has bright lights.
3. A wheel is a round shape.
4. He took a photo of the elephant at the zoo.
5. She blew the whistle to start the game.

Word Book

- Encourage the children to add new or challenging words to *My Third Word Book*.

Answers

Introductory Pupil Book

pages 34–35

Getting started

1. Write a word to name each picture.
   a) *wheat*　　b) *whistle*　　c) *whiskers*
   d) *whale*　　e) *whip*　　f) *wheel*

2. Use the Look, Say, Cover, Write, Check method to learn to spell these question words.

3. Write one question using each word.
   Children's own answers, for example:
   What time is it?
   Where are we going?
   Why are the boys running?
   When will tea be ready?

More to think about

Complete these words using the letters *ph* to make the sound *f*.

1. dolphin　　2. *alphabet*　　3. *photograph*

4. *elephant*　　5. *telephone*　　6. *graph*

Now try these

Use the clues to work out the words starting with the letters *ch*. Hint: you might need to use a capital letter for one word.

1. a shop where you can buy medicine　*chemist*
2. a person in a story　*character*
3. a Christian festival held on 25 December　*Christmas*

Introductory Practice Book

page 13

A　1. dolphin　　　　2. *elephant*
　　3. *photograph*　　4. *telephone*
　　5. *graph*　　　　6. *alphabet*

B　*(Children's own answers.)*

Unit 15

Compound words

Planning

- **Unit focus**
  To split familiar oral and written compound words into their component parts

- **Learning objective**
  Spell with increasing accuracy and confidence, drawing on word recognition and knowledge of word structure

- **Support for Spelling**
  Y2 Term 2 (i): To split compound words into their component parts and to use this knowledge to support spelling

- **Grammar, Punctuation and Spelling Test reference**
  sg/ga7.6

  CPL: Big Book 2B Unit 5 Butterfly Life Cycle

Introduction

Overview

This unit builds upon and consolidates a programme of discrete phonic teaching.

By the end of the unit, the children should be secure in their knowledge and understanding that compound words can be split into component parts.

Rule

Compound words are two small words that join to make one:

wall + paper = wallpaper.

Revisit–Explain–Use

- Ask the children if any of their road/street names combine two words to make one word, for example, Merryburn, Overdale, Westhill, Greenbank.

- Explain to the children that when two words are combined together to form one word, it is called a compound word.

Teach–Model–Define

Word list 15

- Read aloud the sentence: 'When I went into the playground at playtime, I played football.' Invite the children to identify the two words in each compound word: playground, playtime, football.

- Give out a simple word written on card to each child. Ask the children to find a partner to make a compound word using the two words they have brought together. Repeat this activity until plenty of compound words have been made.

  Examples
  play, ground, time, farm, house, yard, arm, wheel, chair, sea, side, foot, net, ball, up, down, stairs, day, time, break, night

- Emphasise the term 'compound word' and establish that a compound word consists of two smaller words joined together to make one word.

- Give practice in spelling simple compound words. Encourage the children to split compound words into their component parts for spelling – clapping the two words.

  Examples
  sunlight, seaside, snowman, manhunt

- Demonstrate the spelling of compound words (for example, daylight), clap for each word. Draw two boxes and write the words in the two boxes, explaining aloud what you are doing.

Practise–Explore–Investigate

- Invite the children to generate compound words from a given root word.

Examples

hair	**post**
hairbrush	postman
haircut	postbox
hairstyle	postbag
	postcard
	postcode

snow	**some**
snowball	someone
snowflake	somebody
snowman	somewhere
snowstorm	somehow

light	**where**
sunlight	somewhere
moonlight	everywhere
daylight	nowhere
starlight	anywhere
searchlight	

- Organise a 'Compound word hunt'. Challenge the children, in groups or pairs, to find as many compound words as they can in a page of text.

Introductory Pupil Book

pages 36–37

Introductory Practice Book

page 14

Resource Sheet 15

Apply–Assess–Reflect

- Give the children the opportunity to reflect on their learning.

- Elicit the key point:
  - a compound word consists of two smaller words joined together to make one word (encourage the children to give examples).

- Ask the children to write two examples of compound words.

Dictation

1. Snowflakes were falling everywhere.
2. I have new wallpaper in my bedroom.
3. My handbag is upstairs.
4. Everyone played in the playground at playtime.
5. My toothbrush is in the bathroom.

Word Book

- Encourage the children to add new or challenging words to *My Third Word Book*.

Answers

Introductory Pupil Book

pages 36–37

Getting started

Join two small words to make one compound word.

1. foot + ball = football
2. black + bird = *blackbird*
3. cow + boy = *cowboy*
4. down + stairs = *downstairs*
5. snow + flake = *snowflake*
6. post + box = *postbox*
7. sea + side = *seaside*
8. skate + board = *skateboard*
9. tea + pot = *teapot*
10. shoe + lace = *shoelace*
11. bed + room = *bedroom*
12. rain + bow = *rainbow*
13. dust + bin = *dustbin*
14. lady + bird = *ladybird*

More to think about

Copy and complete the table.

Compound word	Two small words
greenhouse	green + house
postcard	*post + card*
screwdriver	*screw + driver*
seaweed	*sea + weed*
sunshine	*sun + shine*
homework	*home + work*
somebody	*some + body*
cloakroom	*cloak + room*
grandmother	*grand + mother*
penknife	*pen + knife*

Now try these

Which compound words are these?

1. *hand + bag* = handbag
2. *ear + ring* = earring
3. *sun + flower* = sunflower
4. *suit + case* = suitcase

Introductory Practice Book

page 14

bathroom, *lighthouse, wheelchair, ladybird, something, suitcase, earring, strawberry*

Resource Sheet 15

1. teaspoon
2. *ladybird*
3. *grandmother*
4. *seesaw*
5. *supermarket*
6. *handwriting*
7. *upstairs*
8. *firework*
9. *forget*
10. *butterfly*

Unit 16 Syllables

Planning

- **Unit focus**

  To discriminate syllables in spoken multi-syllable words and to discriminate and identify syllables in written words

- **Learning objective**

  Read and spell phonically decodable two syllable and three syllable words

- **Support for Spelling**

  Y2 Term 3 (ii): To discriminate syllables in multisyllabic words as an aid to spelling

  ---

  CPL: Big Book 2B Unit 5 Butterfly Life Cycle
  CPL: Big Book 2B Unit 6 Spaghetti! Spaghetti!

Introduction

Overview

This unit builds upon and consolidates a programme of discrete phonic teaching.

By the end of the unit, the children should be secure in their knowledge and understanding of the identification of syllables in words and how splitting words into syllables helps with spelling.

Rule

Each beat in a word is a syllable:

teach / er
↑   ↑
syllable 1   syllable 2

Revisit–Explain–Use

- Say a name and then clap the syllables, for example, Pamela, Ahmed, Kate, Sophie, Matilda, Narinder, Adam, Zain.

- Explain that a syllable is a beat, so Kate has one syllable, Sophie has two syllables and Matilda has three syllables.

  Note: It is important that children understand the concept of syllables in words and are alert to using it as a strategy for spelling.

- The following rhyme is useful for reminding children to break words up for spelling. Teach the rhyme to the children and come back to it on other occasions.

  Can't spell a word? Don't be absurd!
  Be proud, says the word out loud
  elephant
  Don't frown just break it down
  el – e – phant
  Be smart, stretch out each part
  e – l – e – ph – a – n – t
  Take a look, take a real good look.

80

Teach–Model–Define

- Say 'banana' and clap the syllables. Now draw lines to show the syllables __ __ __, then write the phonemes for each syllable explaining what you are doing. Write the word 'banana'.

- Give practice in breaking words into syllables and clapping on each syllable. Using these words, encourage the children to practise counting syllables, ask 'How many syllables can you hear?'

  Note: It is important that the words are pronounced clearly and syllables exaggerated.

Word list 16

Examples

garden	magnet	octopus
dinosaur	bedroom	umbrella
messy	banana	book
elephant	traffic	upstairs
wellingtons	bed	photograph

Note: Breaking words into syllables is an important strategy for spelling and children should be encouraged to use it.

Practise–Explore–Investigate

- Invite children to clap the syllables in their names, in colours and in days of the week.

- Ask the children to work in small groups thinking of as many words with two syllables as they can.

  Note: It is important that the children can generate words with two syllables before being asked to write them.

- Repeat for words with three syllables.

Introductory Pupil Book

pages 38–39

Introductory Practice Book

page 15

Resource Sheet 16

A

B

Enrichment

- Investigate with the children words with two syllables that have double consonants, such as rabbit, pepper, summer, butter, traffic, ladder, kennel, funnel. Display words for the children to look at and read. In pairs or small groups, ask the children to find out what all the words have in common and to report back to another pair/group:
  - all words have two syllables
  - all words have double consonants in the middle
  - all words have short vowels.

- Help the children to decide when to use double consonants. In most words with two syllables, if the first vowel is short it is followed by double consonants.

Apply–Assess–Reflect

- Give the children the opportunity to reflect on their learning.

- Elicit the key points:
  - some words can be broken into syllables to help with spelling (encourage the children to give examples and to clap the number of syllables)
  - a syllable is a beat.

- Ask the children to identify the number of syllables heard in words, for example, octopus, rainbow, book, fishing, leg, alphabet.

Dictation

1. I like to eat bananas.

2. The umbrella blew inside out.

3. The train stops when the railway signal is red.

4. I washed my hair with shampoo.

5. I like marmalade on toast.

Word Book

Encourage the children to add new or challenging words to *My Third Word Book*.

Answers

Introductory Pupil Book

pages 38–39

Getting started

Write the words. Mark the syllables. Write the number of syllables in brackets.

1. gar/den   (2)
2. pic/nic   (2)
3. el/e/phant   (3)
4. cray/ons   (2)
5. mag/net   (2)
6. tel/e/scope   (3)
7. ro/bot   (2)
8. pen/ta/gon   (3)
9. cat/er/pil/lar (4)

More to think about

One syllable is missing from a word in each sentence. Add the missing syllables. Write the sentences correctly.

1. The panda was eating bamboo.
2. Ike and Lucy like to play dominoes.
3. Houses made from ice are called igloos.
4. The dragon breathed smoke and flames.
5. There are lots of trees in the garden.
6. Mr Green was sniffing the flower.

Now try these

1. Add the missing syllable to complete each month.
   a) Jan/u/ar/y   b) Feb/ru/ar/y
   c) March   d) Ap/ril
   e) May   f) June
   g) Ju/ly   h) Au/gust
   i) Sep/tem/ber   j) Oc/to/ber
   k) No/vem/ber   l) De/cem/ber

2. Copy and complete the table.

Months with one syllable	Months with two syllables	Months with three syllables	Months with four syllables
March	April	September	January
May	July	October	February
June	August	November	
		December	

Introductory Practice Book

page 15

net,   magnet

et,   jacket

ta,   pasta

ri,   sari

nal,   signal

dile,   crocodile

lin,   violin

Resource Sheet 16

A   1. car/pet   2. gar/den
     3. mag/net   4. lem/on
     5. plan/et   6. win/dow
     7. vel/vet   8. rob/in
     9. bas/ket   10. num/ber

	Word	Number of syllables
B		
1.	puppet	2
2.	rabbit	2
3.	lemonade	3
4.	banana	3
5.	butterfly	3
6.	Wednesday	3

Unit 17

The prefixes *un-* and *dis-*

Planning

- **Unit focus**
  To spell words with common prefixes such as *un-* and *dis-* to indicate the negative

- **Learning objective**
  Spell new words using phonics as the prime approach

- **Support for Spelling**
  Y2 Term 3 (i): To add common prefixes to root words and to understand how they change meaning

- **Grammar, Punctuation and Spelling Test reference**
  sg/ga7.7

  CPL: Big Book 2C Unit 4 A Kiss from a Princess
  CPL: Big Book 2C Unit 4 The Frog Prince

Introduction

Overview

This unit builds upon and consolidates a programme of discrete phonic teaching.

By the end of the unit, the children should be secure in their knowledge and understanding of how adding a prefix to a root word changes its meaning.

Rule

A prefix is a group of letters at the beginning of a word. It can help you work out or change the meaning of a word.

Adding *un-* and *dis-* to words makes the words into their opposites:

un + pack = unpack
dis + obey = disobey.

Revisit–Explain–Use

- Revise the term suffix and invite examples:

  plurals   boy**s**

  past tense   jump**ed**

  present tense   jump**ing**

- Confirm with the children that a suffix is added to the end of a word to change it from singular to plural or from present tense to past tense.

Teach–Model–Define

- Write these words on the board and look at the similarities and differences in each pair of words.

pack	unpack
lock	unlock
happy	unhappy
zip	unzip

- Highlight the part of each word that makes it different from its partner. Ask the children to say what adding *un-* before a word has done to the meaning of the word.

- Establish the following with the children:
  - *un-* is a prefix
  - a prefix is a letter or group of letters added to the beginning of a word to make a new word
  - when *un-* is added to the beginning of many words it gives the word the opposite meaning, for example, able → unable.

- Give practice in writing words with the prefix *un-*. Using individual whiteboards and pens, ask the children to write words that you dictate. Encourage the children to split the words into syllables to help with spelling.

  Examples

unhappy	unzip
unlucky	unlock
untie	unpack
unwell	unable
untidy	

  Note: *Monitor where any errors might occur, with the prefix or with the root word.*

- Introduce the prefix *dis-* which also makes the opposite of the word to which it is added. Illustrate this with words like appear/disappear, trust/distrust, like/dislike, agree/disagree.

- The activities above can be repeated for the new prefix.

Practise–Explore–Investigate

- Give out the prefix cards 'un' and 'dis'. Say words and ask the children to show the correct prefix card that will make the word into its opposite.

  Examples:
  happy, appear, trust, zip, agree, lucky, pack, obey, honest, sure

- Challenge the children to list as many words as they can starting with the prefix *un-*.

- Ask them to exchange their list with a partner and discuss any misspelled words to arrive at the correct spelling. Encourage children to refer back to the rule.

Introductory Pupil Book

pages 40–41

Introductory Practice Book

page 16

Enrichment

- Investigate with the children another common prefix such as *re-*. Ask the children to look at any posters/leaflets within the school about recycling. Discuss the meaning of the prefix *re-* (it means again). Discuss the words 'refill' and 'reuse' in this context.

- Ask the children to work in pairs to generate as many words as possible using the prefix *re-*.

  Possible words:

re + take	*re* + visit
re + play	*re* + write
re + tell	*re* + place
re + build	*re* + heat

Apply–Assess–Reflect AfL

- Give the children the opportunity to reflect on their learning.
- Elicit the key points:
  - *un-* and *dis-* are prefixes
  - prefixes are added to the beginning of words (encourage children to give examples)
  - adding a prefix to a word changes the meaning of the word.
- Ask the children to write one word with the prefix *un-* and one word with the prefix *dis-*.

Dictation

1. I was unwell last Wednesday.
2. He is unable to visit her next week.
3. I had to unlock my case to get my notebook.
4. The classroom is untidy.
5. I dislike the smell of fish.

Word Book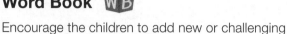

Encourage the children to add new or challenging words to *My Third Word Book*.

Answers

Introductory Pupil Book

pages 40–41

Getting started

1. Copy these words. Underline the prefix in each one.
   a) <u>un</u>zip   b) <u>un</u>lock   c) <u>dis</u>like
   d) <u>un</u>happy   e) <u>dis</u>appear   f) <u>dis</u>agree

2. Write the words from Question 1 again. Then write their opposites.
   a) unzip → zip
   b) unlock → lock
   c) dislike → like
   d) unhappy → happy
   e) disappear → appear
   f) disagree → agree

More to think about

Add the prefix *un-* to make a new word.

1. un + tidy = *untidy*
2. un + load = *unload*
3. un + even = *uneven*
4. un + true = *untrue*
5. un + dress = *undress*
6. un + kind = *unkind*
7. un + able = *unable*
8. un + lucky = *unlucky*
9. un + fair = *unfair*
10. un + pack = *unpack*
11. un + like = *unlike*
12. un + safe = *unsafe*

Now try these

Choose a word from the box to complete each sentence.

1. A thief is a dishonest person.
2. I *dislike* fish and chips.
3. If you *disobey* the rules you will not be in the team.
4. The sun will *disappear* behind the clouds.
5. Tom and Tina always *disagree* with each other.

Introductory Practice Book

page 16

1. untie
2. *unload*
3. *unsafe*
4. *unlock*
5. *unlucky*
6. *unlike*
7. *unhappy*
8. *uncover*

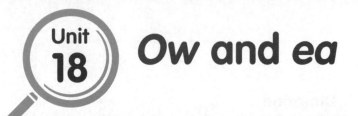

Unit 18 — *Ow* and *ea*

Planning

- **Unit focus**
  To investigate words which have the same spelling patterns but different sounds

- **Learning objective**
  Spell new words using phonics as the prime approach

- **Support for Spelling**
  Y4 Term 2 (i): To investigate and learn to spell words with common letter strings

> **CPL: Big Book 2C** Unit 9 Two Tongue-twisters
> **CPL: Big Book 2C** Unit 9 Riddles

Introduction

Overview

This unit builds upon and consolidates a programme of discrete phonic teaching. By the end of the unit, the children should be secure in their knowledge and understanding of how the same spelling pattern can represent different sounds and that additional text is required to determine pronunciation.

Rule

The letters *ow* can represent different sounds (phonemes): cow, snow.

The letters *ea* can represent different sounds (phonemes): wear, head, dream.

Revisit–Explain–Use

- Revise the long vowel sounds /oa/ and its different representations *oa*, *ow* and *o-e* (see Unit 3).

Teach–Model–Define

Word list 18

- Write words on the board with the letter string *ow* representing different sounds.

  Examples

snow	show
grow	owl
cow	flower
town	now
flow	towel
brown	blow

- Ask the children to tell you what sounds the letters *ow* represent and group the words according to sound.

- Write bow, sow and row on the board and ask the children to read them. Explain that additional text is required to determine the pronunciation of the words. Invite children to give sentences to show the different pronunciations and meanings of the words.

- Give practice in spelling *ow* words. Using individual whiteboards and pens, ask the children to write words in groups that you dictate. This will reinforce letter sequence and motor memory.

- Write words on the board with the letter string *ea* representing different sounds.

  Examples

head	bread
seat	leaf
bear	wear
thread	neat
pear	meal

- Ask the children to tell you what sounds the letters *ea* represent and group the words according to sound.

- Write lead, read and tear on the board and ask the children to read them. Explain that additional text is required to determine the pronunciation of the words. Invite the children to give sentences to show the different pronunciations and meanings of the words.

- Give practice in spelling *ea* words. Using individual whiteboards and pens, ask the children to write words that you dictate.

Practise–Explore–Investigate

- Challenge the children to make lists of words with the letter strings *ea* and *ow*.

- Ask the children to group the words according to the sound the letter string represents.

- Ask the children to exchange their list with a partner and discuss whether the words are placed in the correct groups.

Introductory Pupil Book

pages 42–43

Resource Sheet 18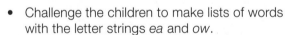

Apply–Assess–Reflect

- Give the children the opportunity to reflect on their learning.

- Elicit the key points:
  - some spelling patterns can represent different sounds (encourage the children to give examples)
  - we need to read the text around the word to know how to pronounce it.

- Ask the children to write two sentences, with the word 'bow' pronounced differently.

- Ask the children to write two sentences, with the word 'tear' pronounced differently in each.

Dictation

1. The bear growled and went to sleep.
2. I had to throw a rope to the man in the boat.
3. The team will wear blue and white shorts.
4. I ate a peach and pear tart.
5. The crown hurt my head.

Word Book

- Encourage the children to add new or challenging words to *My Third Word Book*.

Answers

Introductory Pupil Book

pages 42–43

Getting started

Add *ow* to complete each word.

1. crow
2. *clown*
3. *pillow*
4. *flower*
5. *row*
6. *owl*
7. *shadow*
8. *towel*
9. *mow*

More to think about

Add *ea* to complete each word.

1. pear
2. *peach*
3. *spear*
4. *seal*
5. *bread*
6. *bear*
7. *beads*
8. *thread*
9. *tread*

Now try these

1. Read these two sentences aloud.
   a) The dog has a new <u>lead</u>.
   b) I <u>read</u> my library book last night.

2. Now use the underlined words in Question 1 to complete these rhymes.
   a) *Read* rhymes with *head*.
   b) *Lead* rhymes with *bead*.

Resource Sheet 18

sounds like peach	sounds like bread	sounds like pear
teach	read	wear
beach	head	bear
reach	thread	tear

Unit 19 — The suffixes *-ful* and *-ly*

Planning

- **Unit focus**
  To spell words with the common suffixes *-ful* and *-ly*

- **Learning objective**
  Use knowledge of common inflections in spelling

- **Support for Spelling**
  Y2 Term 2 (ii): To learn how to add common suffixes to words

- **Grammar, Punctuation and Spelling Test reference**
  sg/ga7.8

> **CPL: Big Book 2B** Unit 7 Jill Murphy

Introduction

Overview

This unit builds upon and consolidates a programme of discrete phonic teaching. By the end of the unit, the children should be secure in their knowledge and understanding that adding a suffix to the end of a word makes a new word (adjective).

Rule

A suffix is added to the end of a word to make a new word:

forget	+	ful	=	forgetful
↑		↑		↑
word		suffix		new word

Revisit–Explain–Use

- Revise previous learning with reference to suffixes (inflections) – see Units 11 and 12:
  - adding *-s* to a noun to change singular to plural, for example, boat → boats
  - adding *-ing/ed* to change the tense of a verb, for example, cook → cooking → cooked.

Teach–Model–Define

Word list 19

- Write the following words on the board and look at the similarities and differences in each pair of words.

hand	handful
care	careful
help	helpful
forget	forgetful
use	useful
pain	painful

- Highlight the part of each word that makes it different from its partner. Establish the following with the children:
  - *ful* is a suffix
  - only one letter 'l' is needed when -*ful* is a suffix
  - a suffix is a group of letters added to the end of a word to make a new word.

- Give practice in writing words with the suffix -*ful*. Using individual whiteboards and pens, ask the children to write words that you dictate.

  Note: *Words with suffixes have more than one syllable and children should be encouraged to split words into syllables for spelling. Monitor where errors might occur, with the suffix or with the root word.*

- Introduce the suffix -*ly* and investigate in the same way as -*ful*.

  Examples

safe	safely
love	lovely
slow	slowly
quick	quickly
nice	nicely
soft	softly

Practise–Explore–Investigate

- Challenge the children to list as many words as they can with the suffix -*ful* and the suffix -*ly*.

- In pairs ask the children to group their words according to the suffixes used.

Introductory Pupil Book

pages 44–45

Resource Sheet 19

Enrichment

- Investigate with the children another common suffix such as -*less*. The suffix can be investigated in the same way as -*ful* and -*ly*.

  Examples
  care + *less*
  hope + *less*
  use + *less*
  pain + *less*
  help + *less*

Apply–Assess–Reflect

- Give the children the opportunity to reflect on their learning.

- Elicit the key points:
  - -*ful* and -*ly* are suffixes
  - suffixes are added to the end of words (encourage the children to give examples).

- Ask the children to write one word with the suffix -*ful* and one word with the suffix -*ly*.

Dictation

1. He was careful lifting the jam tarts.
2. She spoke clearly and loudly.
3. She crossed the road safely.
4. Gran has a painful cut on her arm.
5. A spade is a useful garden tool.

Word Book

- Encourage the children to add new or challenging words to *My Third Word Book*.

Answers

Introductory Pupil Book

pages 44–45

Getting started

1. Add the suffix -*ful* to make a new word.
   a) help + ful = helpful
   b) pain + ful = *painful*
   c) hand + full = *handful*
   d) care + ful = *careful*
   e) use + ful = *useful*
   f) hope + ful = *hopeful*
   g) play + ful = *playful*

2. Choose two words from Question 1. Write a sentence using each one.
   (*Children's own answers.*)

More to think about

Add the suffix -*ly* to make new a word.

1. smart + ly = smartly
2. lone + ly = *lonely*
3. quick + ly = *quickly*
4. love + ly = *lovely*
5. slow + ly = *slowly*
6. safe + ly = *safely*
7. calm + ly = *calmly*
8. like + ly = *likely*
9. loud + ly = *loudly*
10. nice + ly = *nicely*
11. friend + ly = *friendly*
12. sure + ly = *surely*

Now try these

Choose the correct word to fill each gap.

1. a) The car drove slowly along the street.
   b) The car is very *slow*.

2. a) Take good *care* of your bike.
   b) He was *careful* when he rode his bike.

3. a) Tariq has a *painful* cut on his foot.
   b) The *pain* in my foot is getting better.

4. a) I hope you have a *safe* journey.
   b) He crossed the road *safely*.

Resource Sheet 19

1. wonder + ful = wonderful
2. thick + *ly* = *thickly*
3. quick + *ly* = *quickly*
4. care + *ful* = *careful*
5. soft + *ly* = *softly*
6. help + *ful* = *helpful*
7. use + *ful* = *useful*
8. spite + *ful* = *spiteful*
9. slow + *ly* = *slowly*
10. love + *ly* = *lovely*
11. lone + *ly* = *lonely*
12. spoon + *ful* = *spoonful*

Progress Unit 3

Answers

A Write a word to name each picture.

1. *fork*
2. *bird*
3. *church*
4. *chair*
5. *spear*
6. *kerb*

B Write a word to name each picture.

1. *dolphin*
2. *bread*
3. *graph*
4. *whip*
5. *whale*
6. *beads*

C Write the words and mark the syllables.
Then count the syllables and write the number in brackets.

1. *drag/on*   (2)
2. *crack/er*   (2)
3. *choc/o/late*   (3)
4. *ham/ster*   (2)
5. *wheel/bar/row*   (3)
6. *croc/o/dile*   (3)

D

1. Choose the correct prefix to make a new word.
   a) *un*lock   b) *dis*obey
   c) *un*kind   d) *dis*like
   e) *dis*loyal   f) *un*wind
   g) *dis*trust   h) *un*lit

2. Choose the correct suffix to make a new word.
   a) slow*ly*   b) care*ful*
   c) love*ly*   d) hope*ful*
   e) like*ly*   f) help*ful*

Spellchecker

Answers

Write these signs correctly. Then check the spellings in your dictionary.

1. *Keep* off the grass
2. *Church* car *park*
3. Buckets and *spades*
4. Do not *feed* the ducks
5. Menu: *roast* beef or fish *pie*
6. *Boats* for hire
7. M8 *South*

Resource sheets

The alphabet

Name _____   **Date** _____

A Write the letters of the alphabet in order.
    Circle the vowels.

_____

_____

B Change the vowel to make new words.
    Write the words.

1. cat   c_u_t   c_o_t   _cat_   _cut_   _cot_

2. not   n___t   n___t   _____   _____   _____

3. beg   b___g   b___g   _____   _____   _____

4. jug   j___g   j___g   _____   _____   _____

5. fin   f___n   f___n   _____   _____   _____

C Change the final consonant to make new words.
    Write the words.

1. ham   ha_t_   ha_d_   _ham_   _hat_   _had_

2. hip   hi___   hi___   _____   _____   _____

3. wed   we___   we___   _____   _____   _____

4. rot   ro___   ro___   _____   _____   _____

Complete the rule

There are _____ letters in the alphabet.

There are _____ vowels. They are *a*, *e*, *i*, *o* and *u*.

The other letters are called _____.

All words have a vowel or the letter ___ in them.

Unit 2 — The long vowel sound *a*

Name _____ **Date** _____

A Write the words for these pictures. Circle the letters that make the long vowel sound *a*.

1.  ___tr(ay)___
2.   _____
3.  _____

4.   _____
5.  _____
6.   _____

7.  _____
8.   _____
9.   _____

B Write three rhyming words in each box.

wake	pain	may
cake	_____	_____
_____	_____	_____
_____	_____	_____

Complete the rule

The long vowel sound *a* can be spelled in different ways:

ai as in *rain* and _____

a_e as in _____

ay as in _____.

The long vowel sound o

Name _____ **Date** _____

A Write the words for these pictures.
Circle the letters that make the long vowel sound o.

1.
   bl(ow)

2.
   _____

3.
   _____

4.
   _____

5.
   _____

6.
   _____

7.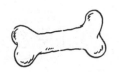
   _____

8.
   _____

9.
   _____

B Write three rhyming words in each box.

float	mole	crow
boat		

Complete the rule

The long vowel sound o can be spelled in different ways:

oa as in boat and _____

o_e as in _____

ow as in _____ .

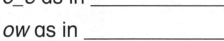

The long vowel sound *e*

Name _____   **Date** _____

A Write the words for these pictures.
Circle the letters that make the long vowel sound *e*.

1.

   l(ee)k _____

2.

   _____

3.

   _____

4.

   _____

5.

   _____

6.

   _____

7.

   _____

8.

   _____

9.

   _____

B Write three rhyming words in each box.

deep	heat
sleep	_____
_____	_____
_____	_____

Complete the rule

The long vowel sound *e* can be spelled in different ways:

ea as in seat and _____

ee as in _____ .

The long vowel sound *u*

Name _____ Date _____

A Find 16 words with the long vowel sound *u*.
Circle the words.

x	b	l	u	e	z	m	u	l	e
d	r	e	w	a	e	f	o	o	d
c	m	c	r	e	w	g	w	h	b
f	j	g	l	u	e	z	n	e	w
p	h	o	o	t	n	r	o	o	t
o	t	r	u	e	p	f	u	m	e
r	u	w	p	r	u	n	e	q	i
z	v	c	l	u	e	m	f	e	w
t	u	n	e	z	h	o	o	f	x

B Write each word in the correct list.

spelled *ue*	spelled *oo*	spelled *ew*	spelled *u_e*
blue			
_____	_____	_____	_____
_____	_____	_____	_____
_____	_____	_____	_____

Complete the rule

The long vowel sound *u* can be spelled in different ways:

oo as in moon and _____   *ue* as in _____

ew as in _____   *u_e* as in _____.

The long vowel sound *i*

Name _____   **Date** _____

A **Write the words for these pictures.**
    Circle the letters that make the long vowel sound *i*.

1. l(igh)t

2. _____

3. _____

4. _____

5. _____

6. _____

B **The words for these clues contain the long vowel sound *i*.**
    Write the words.

1. a journey through the air by a bird or an aircraft   f_____

2. something that has no liquid on it is   d_____

3. when humans, animals or plants stop living
    they do this   d_____

4. we measure this in seconds, minutes, hours,
    days, weeks, months and years   t_____

Complete the rule

The long vowel sound *i* can be spelled in different ways:

ie as in lie and _____

i_e as in _____

igh as in _____

y as in _____.

Oo and u

Name _____   **Date** _____

Find ten words that contain
the letters *oo* or *u* in the boot.
Circle the words.
Write each word in the
correct column.

p	u	l	l	a
b	e	p	u	t
w	o	o	l	c
t	p	u	s	h

f	j	b	o	o	k	d	f	o	o	t
h	r	v	f	u	l	l	k	q	n	g
g	o	o	d	t	y	s	b	u	l	l
m	l	s	t	o	o	d	x	i	z	w

contains *oo*
wool
_____
_____
_____
_____

contains *u*
_____
_____
_____
_____
_____

Complete the rule

The letters *oo* and *u* often make the same sound:

oo as in crook and _____

u as in _____.

Ou and ow

Name _____   Date _____

Some words in the signs have been spelled incorrectly.
Circle the incorrect words.
Write the words correctly.

1. Barn (Ouls)
   <u>owls</u>

2. Trowt Fishing
   _____

3. Scowt Hut
   _____

4. Today's weather Clowds and Rain
   _____

5. aeiou the 5 vouls
   _____

6. Grownd Coffee
   _____

7. Croun Jewels
   _____

8. Flours for Sale
   _____

Complete the rule

The letters *ou* and *ow* can make the same sound:

ou as in house and _____

ow as in _____ .

Adding -*s*

Name _____ **Date** _____

Write the words for these pictures.
The first one has been done for you.

1.

   cat   cats

2.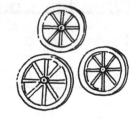

   _____   _____

3.

   _____   _____

4.

   _____   _____

5.

   _____   _____

6.

   _____   _____

7.

   _____   _____

8.

   _____   _____

Complete the rule

For most words just add _____ to make the plural:

dog + _____ = _____.

www.collinseducation.com © HarperCollins*Publishers* Limited 2011

Adding -ed and -ing

Name _____ **Date** _____

Complete each sentence using a word that ends in *-ed* or *-ing*.

1.

   He is k<u>icking</u>____.

2.

   She p_____ the bulbs.

3.

   He sh_____ to me.

4.

   They are r_____.

5.

   She is j_____.

6.

   They c_____ a meal.

7.

   She l_____ the box.

8.

   She is p_____.

Complete the rule

For most words just _____ *-ed* or *-ing*:

sort + *ed* = _____

sort + *ing* = _____.

Or, er, ir, ur, air and ear

Name _____ **Date** _____

Find 12 words hidden in the word search.
Each word contains the letter string *-or*, *-ir*, *-air* or *-ear*.
Circle the words. Write each word in the correct column.

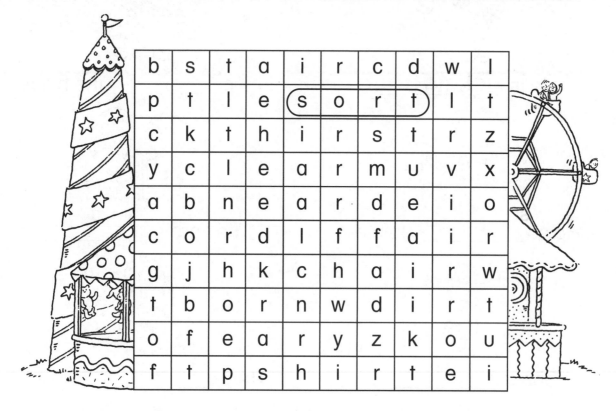

b	s	t	a	i	r	c	d	w	l
p	t	l	e	s	o	r	t	l	t
c	k	t	h	i	r	s	t	r	z
y	c	l	e	a	r	m	u	v	x
a	b	n	e	a	r	d	e	i	o
c	o	r	d	l	f	f	a	i	r
g	j	h	k	c	h	a	i	r	w
t	b	o	r	n	w	d	i	r	t
o	f	e	a	r	y	z	k	o	u
f	t	p	s	h	i	r	t	e	i

contains *-or*	contains *-ir*	contains *-air*	contains *-ear*
sort			

Complete the rule

A letter string is a group of _____ in a word.

Common letter strings are *or*, *ir*, _____ and _____.

Compound words

Unit 15

Name _____   Date _____

Football is a compound word.

foot + ball = football

Join words on the left with words on the right to make compound words. You may only use each word once. Write the compound words.

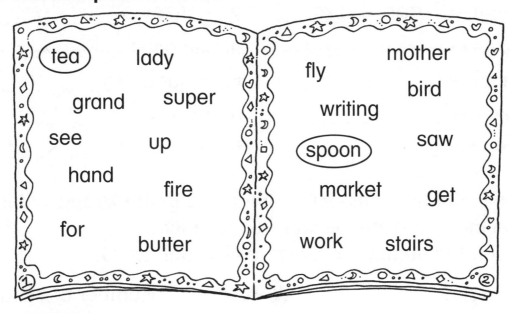

tea   lady

grand   super

see   up

hand

           fire

for

           butter

                    mother

        fly

                       bird

          writing

spoon   saw

          market   get

        work   stairs

1. _teaspoon_   2. _____

3. _____   4. _____

5. _____   6. _____

7. _____   8. _____

9. _____   10. _____

Complete the rule

Compound words are _____ whole words that join to make one:

push + chair = _____.

Syllables

Name _____   **Date** _____

The word picnic has two syllables.

pic/nic

A **Write the words to show the syllables.**
The first one has been done for you.

1. carpet → _car_ / _pet_   2. garden → _____/_____

3. magnet → _____/_____   4. lemon → _____/_____

5. planet → _____/_____   6. window → _____/_____

7. velvet → _____/_____   8. robin → _____/_____

9. basket → _____/_____   10. number → _____/_____

B **The syllables in the left column are in the wrong order.**
Use them to write the words correctly.
Count the number of syllables in each word.

Syllables	Word	Number of syllables
1. pet / pup	_puppet_	_2_
2. bit / rab	_____	_____
3. on / lem / ade	_____	_____
4. na / na / ba	_____	_____
5. ter / fly / but	_____	_____
6. day / nes / Wed	_____	_____

Complete the rule

Each beat in a word is a _____.

customer = cus/_____/_____.

www.collinseducation.com © HarperCollins*Publishers* Limited 2011

Ow and ea

Name _____ Date _____

Make nine words with *ea* in the middle.
Take a letter from the first wing and use it to start the word.
Take a letter from the second wing and use it to end
the word.

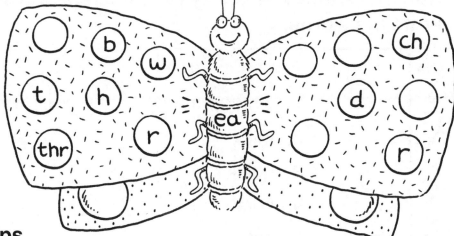

Write the words
in rhyming groups.

sounds like peach	sounds like bread	sounds like pear
_____	_____	_____
_____	_____	_____
_____	_____	_____

Complete the rule

The letters *ea* can make different sounds:

air as in wear

_____ as in head

_____ as in dream.

The suffixes -*ful* and -*ly*

Name _____ Date _____

-*ly* is a suffix.

slow + ly = slowly

**Add the suffixes -*ful* or -*ly* to make new words.
Write the words.**

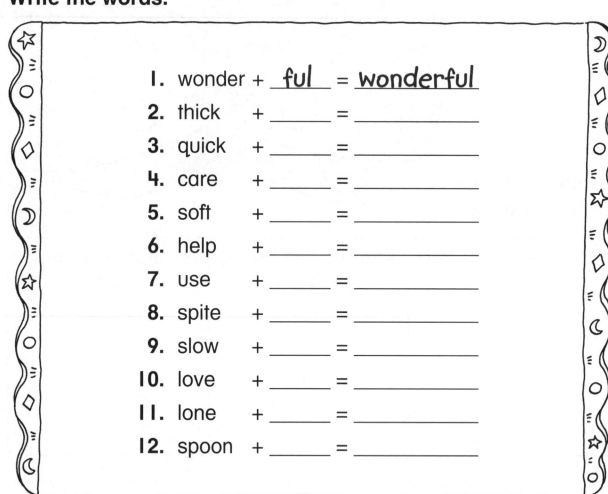

1. wonder + <u>ful</u> = <u>wonderful</u>
2. thick + _____ = _____
3. quick + _____ = _____
4. care   + _____ = _____
5. soft   + _____ = _____
6. help   + _____ = _____
7. use   + _____ = _____
8. spite + _____ = _____
9. slow   + _____ = _____
10. love + _____ = _____
11. lone + _____ = _____
12. spoon + _____ = _____

Complete the rule

A suffix is a group of letters added to the _____ of a word
to make a new word:

care + ful = _____.

Word lists

a_e words

bake	came	ate	fade	cave	sale	daze	tape
cake	fame	date	made	gave	tale	maze	grape
lake	game	gate	spade	save	male	blaze	shape
make	lame	hate	trade	rave	whale		
take	same	mate		wave	stale		
wake	tame	plate		grave			
flake	shame	skate		brave			
snake	flame	grate		shave			
shake		crate		slave			

cane	safe	case
mane		chase
pane		

ai words

fail	laid	gain	wait	faint
hail	paid	rain	waist	paint
jail	raid	pain		
mail		stain		
nail		train		
pail		grain		
rail		brain		
sail		Spain		
tail		chain		
snail				
trail				

ay words

bay	clay	day	play	tray	lay	stay
hay	fray	may	sway	pay	pray	ray
say	way	slay				

oa words

oat	coal	load	loan	coast	oak	soap	loaf
boat	foal	road	moan	roast	soak	coach	foam
coat	goal	toad	groan	toast	cloak		
goat	shoal			boast			
moat							
float							
stoat							
throat							

o_e words

hole	coke	hose	bone	hope	code
mole	joke	nose	cone	rope	rode
pole	poke	rose	stone	slope	
sole	woke	close	throne		
stole	broke	chose			
	spoke				
	smoke				
	choke				

ow words

bow	blow	arrow	shallow	elbow
low	snow	narrow	follow	window
mow	flow	barrow	yellow	shadow
row	glow	sparrow	pillow	
sow	grow			
tow	crow			
throw				
know				

Word list
The long vowel sound e

ea words

eat	seam	bean	meal	each	bead
heat	team	lean	seal	teach	lead
beat	cream	mean	real	reach	read
meat	dream		steal	beach	
seat	steam			peach	
pleat	stream				
bleat	scream				
wheat					
treat					

ee words

bee	beef	feel	deep	feet	need	week	teeth
see	reef	heel	keep	meet	weed	seek	
tree		peel	peep	sleet	seed	leek	
free		reel	weep	sweet	feed	meek	
three		steel	steep	greet	tweed	cheek	
knee		wheel	sleep	sheet	greed	sleek	
		kneel	bleep		breed		
			cheep		speed		
			sheep		bleed		
			creep				

Word list
The long vowel sound *u*

oo words

moon	food	boot	troop	wool	gloom	too	hoof
noon	mood	hoot	stoop	fool	bloom	zoo	
soon		root	scoop	pool	broom		
spoon		shoot	droop	stool	groom		
afternoon			toot	hoop	spool	room	
		scoot	loop	school	zoom		
				cool			
				tool			

ew words

dew	flew	threw
few	blew	knew
new	grew	screw
pew	crew	chew
	drew	
	stew	

ue words

blue
true
clue
glue

u_e words

cube	mule	use	June	cute
tube	rule	fuse	tune	jute
			prune	flute

Word list
The long vowel sound *i*

ie words

lie	pie	die	tie

igh words

high	fight
sigh	might
thigh	light
	night
	right
	sight
	tight
	bright
	flight
	fright

i_e words

hide	pipe	dine	mime	file	bite	bike	wife
ride	ripe	fine	time	pile	kite	like	knife
tide	wipe	line	chime	tile	white		
side	swipe	mine	crime	mile			
wide	tripe	nine	grime	smile			
slide		pine		while			
bride		wine		stile			
		twine					
		spine					
		shine					
		swine					

y words

cry	my	fly	sky
dry	by	sly	sty
fry			spy
try			why
			shy

www.collinseducation.com © HarperCollins*Publishers* Limited 2011

Word list
Oo and u

oo words	**u words**	
stood	bull	put
hood	pull	push
good	full	
wood	bully	
brook	fully	
hook		
took		
book		
cook		
look		
shook		
wool		
foot		

Word list
Words with *ar*

car	art	arm	yarn	ark	card	harp
bar	dart	farm	barn	park	hard	sharp
jar	cart	harm	darn	bark	lard	
far	part			dark	yard	
tar	tart			hark		
star	start			lark		
	chart			mark		
				spark		
				shark		

www.collinseducation.com © HarperCollins*Publishers* Limited 2011

Word list
Oi and *oy*

oi words

coin	joint	moist	oil
join	point	hoist	boil
		joist	soil
			coil
			toil
			spoil
			foil

oy words

coy	annoy
boy	enjoy
joy	cowboy
toy	tomboy

Word list
Ou and ow

ou words

loud	found	mouth	grout	count	foul	house
cloud	hound	south	snout	mount		mouse
proud	mound		stout			
	round		trout			
	pound		spout			
	sound		scout			
	ground		shout			
	wound					

ow words

bow	town	owl	towel	tower	crowd
cow	down	fowl	vowel	power	
how	gown	growl	trowel	flower	
row	frown	howl		shower	
now	drown			powder	
	brown				
	crown				

Word list
Adding -s

bags	lids	dogs	jets	buns
dads	pigs	mops	legs	tubs
fans	fins	dots	pegs	mugs
cats	zips	rods	hens	cups
vans	bibs	cots	beds	huts

frogs	stems	cuffs	ships	plates	boats
prams	slugs	sniffs	sheds	trains	roads
traps	grins	drills	shops	days	crows
crabs	plans	smells	chips	chains	cones
drips	flags	shells	chops	gates	bones

sweets	brooms	ties	books	cars
beads	screws	kites	hooks	sharks
seals	flutes	slides	bulls	cards
wheels	cubes	pies	cooks	parks

coins	crowns
boys	clouds
toys	owls
boils	sounds

Word list
Adding -ed and -ing

talk	→	talked	→	talking
peck	→	pecked	→	pecking
lick	→	licked	→	licking
lift	→	lifted	→	lifting
open	→	opened	→	opening
push	→	pushed	→	pushing
rain	→	rained	→	raining
bark	→	barked	→	barking
groan	→	groaned	→	groaning
pull	→	pulled	→	pulling
play	→	played	→	playing
cook	→	cooked	→	cooking
rock	→	rocked	→	rocking
melt	→	melted	→	melting
start	→	started	→	starting
peel	→	peeled	→	peeling
shout	→	shouted	→	shouting
point	→	pointed	→	pointing
snow	→	snowed	→	snowing
dust	→	dusted	→	dusting

Word list
Or, er, ir, ur, air and ear

or words

horn	fork	cord	sort	storm
corn	cork	lord	snort	
born	York		short	
morn	stork			
torn				
thorn				

er words

her	herd	perch	fern	term

ir words

bird	twirl	first	dirt	birth	smirk
third	whirl	thirst	skirt	mirth	chirp
	swirl		shirt		
			squirt		

ur words

curl	urn	burst
hurl	burn	blur
furl	turn	church
		hurt

air words

air	fair	hair	stair	chair

ear words

ear	fear	dear	gear	hear
near	tear	spear	clear	shear

www.collinseducation.com © HarperCollins*Publishers* Limited 2011

Word list
Wh, ph and ch

wh words

when	wheat
whip	whistle
whisk	whiskers
whiff	whisper
which	wheel
what	whip
where	whirl
why	whale

ph words

phone

dolphin

elephant

alphabet

graph

photograph

nephew

orphan

ch words

chin	chain	chemist	chef
chip	cheek	chorus	chiffon
chap	cheat	Christmas	chute
chop	chew	character	machine
chimp	chart		parachute
champ	charm		
chest	chair		
chick	church		

Word list
Compound words

butterfly	screwdriver	goalpost
daylight	grasshopper	waistcoat
snowboard	earring	handbag
raincoat	upstairs	fireplace
snowman	hairbrush	seesaw
toothbrush	postman	football
childhood	teaspoon	lighthouse
tablecloth	footpath	bookcase

Word list Syllables

candle	kettle	bucket
curtain	picnic	octopus
table	wooden	teddy
shopping	kitten	banana
garden	window	children
jelly	puppet	elephant
rabbit	basket	pencil
kitchen	dragon	dinosaur
alphabet	sofa	rubber
mummy	acrobat	lion
person	bandage	teacher
wallet	domino	caterpillar

www.collinseducation.com © HarperCollins*Publishers* Limited 2011

Word list
The prefixes *un-* and *dis-*

un words

unwell	undone	uneven
unable	unlock	undress
unsure	unhappy	unfair
untie	unlike	unsafe
unpack	untidy	unload

dis words

disappear

disobey

distrust

disagree

dishonest

Word list
Ow and ea

ow words

cow	owl	bow	arrow
bow	fowl	low	narrow
how	growl	mow	barrow
row		row	sparrow
now	towel	snow	
sow	vowel	blow	shadow
		flow	elbow
town	tower	glow	
gown	power	grow	follow
frown	flower	crow	yellow
drown	shower	show	pillow
brown	powder	throw	
crown	crowd	know	

ea words

wear	head	eat	meal
bear	bread	heat	seal
pear	tread	meat	real
tear	thread	seat	steal
		pleat	
		bleat	bead
		wheat	read
		bean	each
		lean	reach
		mean	peach
			teach
		team	beach
		seam	
		dream	
		cream	

Word list
The suffixes -*ful* and -*ly*

-*ful* words

helpful

hopeful

useful

careful

handful

spoonful

painful

playful

joyful

-*ly* words

slowly	evenly	smartly
softly	closely	calmly
quickly	safely	loudly
smartly	barely	lonely
likely	lovely	safely
nicely	plainly	
surely	friendly	
loudly		

High-frequency words

The first 100 high-frequency words in order

1. the	26. are	51. do	76. about
2. and	27. up	52. me	77. got
3. a	28. had	53. down	78. their
4. to	29. my	54. dad	79. people
5. said	30. her	55. big	80. your
6. in	31. what	56. when	81. put
7. he	32. there	57. it's	82. could
8. I	33. out	58. see	83. house
9. of	34. this	59. looked	84. old
10. it	35. have	60. very	85. too
11. was	36. went	61. look	86. by
12. you	37. be	62. don't	87. day
13. they	38. like	63. come	88. made
14. on	39. some	64. will	89. time
15. she	40. so	65. into	90. I'm
16. is	41. not	66. back	91. if
17. for	42. then	67. from	92. help
18. at	43. were	68. children	93. Mrs
19. his	44. go	69. him	94. called
20. but	45. little	70. Mr	95. here
21. that	46. as	71. get	96. off
22. with	47. no	72. just	97. asked
23. all	48. mum	73. now	98. saw
24. we	49. one	74. came	99. make
25. can	50. them	75. oh	100. an

Word list from Masterton, J., Stuart, M., Dixon, M. and Lovejoy, S. (2003)
Children's Printed Word Database (accessible at www.essex.ac.uk/psychology/cpwd).
Economic and Social Research Council funded project, R00023406.

The next 200 most common words in order of frequency

This list is read down the columns (i.e. in the list, *water* is most frequently used and *grow* is the least frequently used).

water	yes	lots	suddenly	girl	eggs
away	play	need	told	which	once
good	take	that's	another	inside	please
want	thought	baby	great	run	thing
over	dog	fish	why	any	stopped
how	well	gave	cried	under	ever
did	find	mouse	keep	hat	miss
man	more	something	room	snow	most
going	I'll	bed	last	air	cold
where	round	may	jumped	trees	park
would	tree	still	because	bad	lived
or	magic	found	even	tea	birds
took	shouted	live	am	top	duck
school	us	say	before	eyes	horse
think	other	soon	gran	fell	rabbit
home	food	night	clothes	friends	white
who	fox	narrator	tell	box	coming
didn't	through	small	key	dark	he's
ran	way	car	fun	grandad	river
know	been	couldn't	place	there's	liked
bear	stop	three	mother	looking	giant
can't	must	head	sat	end	looks
again	red	king	boat	than	use
cat	door	town	window	best	along
long	right	I've	sleep	better	plants
things	sea	around	feet	hot	dragon
new	these	every	morning	sun	pulled
after	began	garden	queen	across	we're
wanted	boy	fast	each	gone	fly
eat	animals	only	book	hard	grow
everyone	never	many	its	floppy	
our	next	laughed	green	really	
two	first	let's	different	wind	
has	work	much	let	wish	

Word list from Masterton, J., Stuart, M., Dixon, M. and Lovejoy, S. (2003)
Children's Printed Word Database (accessible at www.essex.ac.uk/psychology/cpwd).
Economic and Social Research Council funded project, R00023406.

Notes